M000032201

Praise for *The Courage Factor*

"Inside *The Courage Factor* is the key to joy. Do you have the courage to boldly pursue it? Let my friend Bob Westfall take you on a journey of discovery—an exciting and fulfilling trek that he traces back two thousand years. Are you intrigued? Then take the challenge! Open the book. Read on with an open heart and mind!"

—Lee Strobel, *New York Times* best-selling author

"It's one thing for a person to possess courage and quite another to inspire others to have it too. Bob Westfall has inspired numerous ministry leaders to conquer their fears, stretch their faith, and set their sights on accomplishing the impossible. Millions of hurting people have received help and found hope because ministry leaders followed the principles found in *The Courage Factor*. Place this book on top of your reading stack—you'll be glad you did."

—Hal Donaldson, president of Convoy of Hope

"*The Courage Factor* stopped me in my tracks. I felt God saying, 'Hey, big shot, I gave you your talent . . . how have you used it for me?' Thanks, Bob, for rocking me *big time*. It's never too late to shoot for the moon and spiritually turn a dime into a dollar."

—John Elefante, former lead singer of Kansas, Grammy and Dove award-winning performer/producer

"In this outstanding book, Bob challenges you to get off the sidelines and get into the game! God takes our gifts and all that we invest and exponentially multiplies it for his purposes. Too often, believers hold back, wondering, 'Am I good enough? Are my gifts compelling enough? Can God use me?' Bob challenges us to step past our fear and start using all we've been given for God's glory, promising that if we do, we will find joy. I highly recommend!"

—Becky Harling, best-selling author of *How to Listen So People Will Talk* and *The 30 Day Praise Challenge*

"By sharing good fortune with others, we foster and build communities of care and respect, uplifting those around us through our good deeds and actions. *The Courage Factor* paints a compelling portrait that details the inherent power of giving."

—Isadore Sharp, founder and chairman of Four Seasons Hotels and Resorts

"I'll never think the same way again about the Parable of the Talents. Bob has defined this parable and, with real stories, makes it jump off the page and come alive in a way I've never heard. This book has etched itself onto me forever. I've seen Bob's program and its effectiveness, and now it's clear where his passion comes from."

—Andrew Covington, president of Dufresne Spencer Group (DBA Ashley Homestores)

"Wonderfully moving, and inspiring, *The Courage Factor* will make you feel like you are in the personal company of its extraordinary author, a man whom I am proud to call a friend. It is also a challenging read, as every story, example, and lesson cajoles the reader to examine their God given talents and urges their full use to faithful purpose. On such a journey, one that can be fraught and testing but ultimately joyous, there can be no better companion than Bob Westfall."

—Simon Majumdar, author and broadcaster

"I am always inspired when someone uses their passion to better the world. No matter your faith, I admire Bob's commitment and determination to bring joy to those around him and to encourage people to use their talents to the best of their ability."

—Alan Fuerstman, founder, chairman, and CEO
of Montage International

"I have personally seen the Westfall Gold model, and the outcomes achieved by Bob and his team, at work. I am a firm believer that each of us is equipped with unique and beautiful talents. As you read this book, I hope you are inspired as I am to use these gifts for the Kingdom."

—Congressman Tim Walberg

The
Courage Factor

The Courage Factor

TAKING BOLD STEPS THAT LEAD TO JOY

by

Bob Westfall

LEAFWOOD PUBLISHERS

2020

The Courage Factor
Taking Bold Steps That Lead to Joy

Copyright © 2020 by Bob Westfall

ISBN 978-1-68426-140-6

Printed in Canada

Library of Congress Cataloging-in-Publication Data

Names: Westfall, Bob, author.
Title: The courage factor : taking bold steps that lead to joy / Bob Westfall.
Description: Abilene, Texas : Leafwood Publishers, [2020]
Identifiers: LCCN 2019057815 | ISBN 9781684261406 (hardcover)
Subjects: LCSH: Self-realization—Religious aspects—Christianity. | Fear—Religious aspects—Christianity. | Courage—Religious aspects—Christianity. | Joy—Religious aspects—Christianity. | Talents (Parable) | Bible. Matthew, XXV, 14–30—Criticism, interpretation, etc.
Classification: LCC BV4598.2 .W447 2020 | DDC 248.4—dc23
LC record available at https://lccn.loc.gov/2019057815

Cover design by ThinkPen Design
Interior text design by Scribe Inc.

Leafwood Publishers is an imprint of Abilene Christian University Press
ACU Box 29138
Abilene, Texas 79699
1-877-816-4455
www.leafwoodpublishers.com

20 21 22 23 24 25 / 7 6 5 4 3 2 1

To my mentor,
Bruce Wilkinson.
It is because of your belief in me,
the investment you made in my life and career,
and the ways in which you've consistently
poured into me that this dream came true.
It would have never been a dream at all
without your friendship.
Thank you, dear friend.

————

To my father and mother,
Robert Westfall and Dixie Wigbels,
not only am I an extension of your magnificent DNA,
but I am also an extension of you two
incredibly beautiful human beings.

Contents

Foreword

No Other Way to Live

Dr. Henry Cloud

I remember it like it was yesterday. My oldest daughter, Olivia, was a preschooler, and we were eating breakfast. As the psychologist father, I had to torture her with another "life lesson," as she has come to call them.

"So, Olivia . . . you know how we have been talking about 'sharing'?"

"Yep, Dad . . . what about it?" she replied.

"I have an idea. Today at school, I want you to find someone and share something with them, and then tonight we can talk about it. Good?" I requested.

"Uh. . . . OK, I will," she answered. I was not very sure what the follow-through would look like, but it was a start.

That night, I asked her, "How did your sharing go? Did you do it?"

"Yes. At snack time, I had two cookies that Mom had given me, and I saw a girl that didn't have any, so I walked over to her table and gave her one of mine," she proudly reported.

"Livi!!! That's awesome!" I congratulated. "How did it go?" I was asking mostly to find out about what kind of response she got. Instead, I got something very different.

"Daddy. . . . what is it?" she asked me.

"What is what?" I quizzed.

"What is it in *here*?" She pointed to her little chest. I did not understand what she was asking.

"What? Where? What do you mean 'in here'?" I asked.

She just repeated and pointed to her chest. "In here? What is it in *here*?"

"Livi, I don't understand. What do you mean 'in here'?"

She looked up. "When I gave her the cookie, it felt really *warm* in here," she answered, again pointing to her chest.

I was stunned. I did not know how to reply. I was breaking up inside, trying to hide the tears as my little girl was discovering what giving does to us, and seeing her experience it in such a profound way. But I did my best to answer at her level.

"That's love, Livi. It's love that you feel in your heart as you see someone else get something good that you gave them. It feels good to share, huh?"

I was trying to stay composed. . . . I even thought of saying, "Well, it is your neurotransmitters responding to a connected experience and aligning with your deepest values and God-given wiring, and you are learning that it is 'more blessed to give than receive.' In fact, Livi, it will extend your life, increase your immune functioning, draw you out of isolation, give you purpose, and overall cause you to thrive in life, this 'giving' thing."

But I didn't say all that, as it would have been just an attempt to keep from shedding my tears of joy as I saw this little creature discover all that God has for us in this little gesture. My prayer was that she would never forget it and would build upon that moment for a lifetime.

"Oh . . . that's really nice. It felt so good," she said, wrapping up the life lesson.

"Keep doing it," I replied. "It only gets better."

"OK, Daddy," she responded.

I wanted to pull out my whiteboard and give her a full download of all that giving does for us, but she was only about four, so I restrained myself. But wow, I really, really wanted to. Even as I write this, I still tear up thinking about that moment in her little life and that now, at nineteen, she is continuing to live as a giver. Who said life lessons don't work?

Today, I wish I could sit with all of you and complete that whiteboard session because giving is so powerful. But as a psychologist, I can truly attest to what I said above. The research about happiness and thriving is clear: *givers are the happiest people*. Health, meaning, connection, thriving, relationships, success, and so many other factors rest on this one life practice—the practice of giving. It was Jesus who said, "It is more blessed to give than to receive" (Acts 20:35). And it seems that the person who wrote the Bible also knew something about the human brain too. Did you know that when you give, the same pleasure centers light up in the brain as when you are eating good food or having great sex? Take out your wallet!

I can attest to all that research as a psychologist and implore you to live a healthy life. But to me, it is more than just being a psychologist that moves me to remind all of us to be givers. It is personal experience as well.

My wife, Tori, and I were both raised to be givers, and fortunately, as a couple, we have always been united in giving and philanthropy. It is one of the most meaningful things we do together, and we love doing it as a team. Together, we have been privileged to speak at many Westfall Gold donor events and have personally had the opportunity to see hundreds of individuals and couples come together as donors to the various charities that Westfall Gold works with. We have been able to witness these givers who live out literal lifetimes of giving and see the fulfillment that they have, just like Olivia did, "in here." We see people whose little hearts are now big hearts, and we see the meaningful lives that they enjoy, having developed the practice and the discipline of sharing their resources with a world in which too many are deprived.

We have seen them change worlds—people have gone from living in diseased communities to receiving health care, from starving to being able to depend on a meal, from drinking muddy, disease-laden water to having available healthy water, or from being young girls sold into sex slavery to being rescued and placed in families that heal them. And the worthy causes are limitless.

And sometimes, it takes courage to step out and give. The courage to step into the "more" that God has for us. The courage to even give "more" than we have ever given before.

Fortunately, I don't need a whiteboard. Bob Westfall has provided a much better seminar here in this book. In these pages, we get to see many examples of what Olivia discovered that day: *it is more blessed to give than to receive.* My prayer is that you find in these fellow travelers a great reminder as they inspire you with their stories. As we all give more, we can, in fact, change the world.

Los Angeles, California, 2019

Preface

The Great Adventure

There's something you want. We all want it. In fact, our hearts ache for it. Some of us realize it sooner than others. Unfortunately, some of us never realize it at all.

It's joy. It's fulfillment. It's a pleasure and contentment and peace that runs deep within our very being.

Do you have it?

The whole purpose of this little book is to tell you that you can have it. You can live in the joy and contentment that we all seek.

Yet there is a secret to this joy. It is a secret that comes at a price. The great truth of the joy I describe in these pages is that it comes on the other side of life-altering courage. Before we can live in the beauty of this secret, we have to commit to something—a kind of purpose, or calling, or perhaps destiny. Really, it is our reason for being. And to pursue it requires great courage and great boldness.

What I am asking you to do in these pages is to come to grips with a big part of what you were made for and then to fiercely step into it. Despite your fears. Despite the storms of opposition. Despite the nagging uncertainties and doubts. I want you to take the bold, courageous steps that will lead to a life-changing joy.

I'm willing to ask this of you because I have taken such steps myself. I'll be honest. It wasn't easy. When I first realized what true joy required of me, I was going through one of the worst times of my life. I was successful in my work, but much else about my life was painful and, in some cases, crumbling.

Yet God chose that time to show me the truths that I'm going to show you in this book. I was changed by them. And then I had the opportunity to introduce others to these same truths. The results have been pretty amazing—and not because I am anything special. They have been amazing because I began living a truth that is special, a truth that comes from God and can be lived out by those who are willing, those who dare to be courageous, and those who break from the norms of our time.

Let me tell you one of the most exciting aspects of the truths I plan to tell you here. It is that the truths are for all of us. They are not just for the famous or the wealthy or the good looking. They are not just for pastors or missionaries or the uniquely gifted. They are truths for all of us, but only the willing end up experiencing them in full. That's why I'm excited to step into this with you. If we do as these truths require, we will begin to live the great adventure we were made for. There is simply nothing else like it.

I have two thoughts for you before we begin. First, I'm completely convinced that God authored the truths I'm eager to show you here and that he led me to them years ago. So in these pages, I'm going to mention God and quote Scripture from time to time. I realize you may not be religious. You may not even be sure there is a God. Still, I want you to stick with me. I want you to hang in until the end and see if these truths don't prove themselves to you. What I'm saying is this: whether you believe in God as I do or not, come along for the ride and see if you don't experience what I did. Trust me, there's some good stuff coming your way!

Finally, I need to say clearly that I'm not the hero of what follows in this book. Nor are the people whose stories I'm going to tell, though all of them have done heroic things that have made a difference in the world. Instead, you are the hero. My goal here is to be your guide, your coach. I'm here to help you understand that true joy awaits you and that courage is the pathway to it. So don't settle back just to be regaled by thrilling tales of accomplishment. Get ready for accomplishments of your own. Get ready for the joy you were made for. Get ready to make the difference you were designed to make. My role is to tell you what I've seen—and help you take courage to soar.

Let's get to it.

Chapter 1

Ancient Words

Hide not your talents, they for use were made. What's a sundial in the shade?

—Benjamin Franklin

S everal decades ago, a dear friend drew my attention to some ancient words. He asked me to read them, to think about them, and to apply them to my life. It is hard to describe, all these years later, how much of a difference that simple request made. Nearly every day of my life, I live out the lasting legacy of that moment.

Before I tell you more about this legacy, I want to tell you what these ancient words are. I trust that as I recount them to you and provide a little explanation, you'll see why they have meant so much to so many through the centuries.

These words were first spoken by Jesus Christ as he taught

his twelve disciples during the days of the Roman Empire. He had been living with his disciples and teaching them for nearly three years by the time he said these words, but his time with them was coming to an end. Jesus had already begun talking about his death, and questions naturally began to form in the minds of his disciples: "How are we going to live without him? What does he expect of us once he's gone?"

Sensing these concerns, Jesus decided to tell them a story. This was often how he communicated truth. It is interesting that brain scientists today tell us that stories are the best way for human beings to absorb truth and to remember it. Jesus obviously knew this, and it is why most of what he taught the world was embedded in stories that we've come to call parables.

One of these is found in the New Testament book of Matthew, in chapter 25 starting with verse 14. This is the one I want to break out for you here, the one that so impacted my life.

Jesus had been discussing the kingdom of God with his disciples just before he launched into his story. Here are the opening words:

> For it [the kingdom of God] will be like a man going on a journey, who called his servants and entrusted to them his property. To one he gave five talents, to another two, to another one, to each according to his ability. Then he went away.

Now, it adds to the drama and symbolism of this story if we know what the word *talent* meant in the time of Jesus. Of course, we use this word in English today to describe something wonderful a person is able to do, like dance or play guitar or cook or speak well in public or perhaps build houses. Yet this meaning of the word *talent* was not the one used in Jesus's day.

Instead, a talent was a certain weight of silver. It was used the way we use words like *pound* or *ounce* or *ton*. So when we are told in the story that a man was given a talent, it doesn't mean he was suddenly given the ability to sing or paint beautifully. Instead, it means he was given a certain amount of silver.

Knowing this really adds understanding to the story, especially since a talent at the time of Jesus would have been about 80 pounds of silver. This was a huge amount, equal in money to what the average man earned in sixteen years of labor. Pretty amazing!

So in the bit of the story we've read so far, the first man was given five talents, or 400 pounds of silver. This equaled what a man at that time would have been paid for 80 years of labor. The second man was given two talents, or 160 pounds of silver, equal to 32 years of labor at the time. And the last man, the one who was given one talent of silver, was entrusted with what we already know: 80 pounds of silver, which was equal to the pay for 16 years of an average man's work.

My reason for exploring all this detail is to help you see that the master in our story entrusted his servants with things of great worth. To bring this into our own time, think about how much money you are likely to make in the next sixteen years. Now double it. Now multiply it by five instead. See what I mean? Each man was told to take care of a huge amount of wealth.

It is also important for us to remember that each man was trusted "according to his own ability." In other words, their master wasn't being cruel. He didn't load them up with more than they could handle. He entrusted them with great wealth to deal with but also wealth that they should have been able to handle given their individual abilities.

Now, armed with this information, let's return to our story:

> He who had received the five talents went at once and traded with them, and he made five talents more. So also he who had the two talents made two talents more. But he who had received the one talent went and dug in the ground and hid his master's money.
>
> Now after a long time the master of those servants came and settled accounts with them.
>
> And he who had received the five talents came forward, bringing five talents more, saying, "Master, you delivered to me five talents; here, I have made five talents more." His master said to him, "Well done,

good and faithful servant. You have been faithful over a little; I will set you over much. Enter into the joy of your master."

And he also who had the two talents came forward, saying, "Master, you delivered to me two talents; here, I have made two talents more." His master said to him, "Well done, good and faithful servant. You have been faithful over a little; I will set you over much. Enter into the joy of your master."

He also who had received the one talent came forward, saying, "Master, I knew you to be a hard man, reaping where you did not sow, and gathering where you scattered no seed, so I was afraid, and I went and hid your talent in the ground. Here, you have what is yours."

But his master answered him, "You wicked and slothful servant! You knew that I reap where I have not sown and gather where I scattered no seed? Then you ought to have invested my money with the bankers, and at my coming I should have received what was my own with interest.

"So take the talent from him and give it to him who has the ten talents. For to everyone who has will more be given, and he will have an abundance. But from the one who has not, even what he has will be taken away. And cast the worthless servant into the outer darkness. In that place there will be weeping and gnashing of teeth." (Matt. 25:14–30)

What an amazing story! Let's dive into its meaning a bit. Each servant was entrusted with a massive amount of silver. Each was given his amount according to his ability. Two of these servants went out and, through wise trading, doubled their master's wealth. The third man, though, gave in to his fear. He says so himself. Terrified as he was, he hid his one talent of silver in the ground, probably so no one would steal it.

Yet when his master returned and found out that he had not increased the value of what was entrusted to him—that he had not created growth and increase—the man was condemned. His master called him "wicked," "lazy," and "worthless." Then the master cast this man into "outer darkness."

Let's keep our eyes on the first two men. They increased their master's wealth. They used their talents to create increase. Their master celebrated them. He said he would give these men positions of even greater responsibility. Then he said the words that changed my life but that we often miss in this story. He told these men they could "enter into the joy of your master."

There they are! Those words that burned in my heart so many years ago. The joy of the master. What a mind-blowing reward!

Now let's zoom out from the details of this story. We've already said that it isn't about talent as we use the word in English today. Yet I should also say that this story isn't really just about money or silver either. Remember what Jesus was talking about when he launched into this story with his disciples? He was talking about the kingdom of God, the rule of God on earth. He was telling them what it would be like once he was gone and how they would be called upon to use whatever God entrusted to them to bring increase, growth, and good for God's purposes.

I believe this is why Jesus used such huge amounts of silver in his story. He wanted us to think about things of great value, things that have been entrusted to us according to our ability to handle them. He wanted us to understand that in the kingdom of God, you have to use what has been entrusted to you, to invest it, or "put it into play" as we often say today, to see it produce results for the good of others.

What kinds of things are we talking about? The short answer is, "Whatever has been entrusted." Vision. Skills. Destined purposes. Wealth. Leadership abilities. Special understanding of a social problem. Deep compassion for the needs of a people. Unique gifts for handling money or investments or an industry or any of a thousand other arenas and pursuits. In other words, you name it! We are talking about whatever valuable things Jesus has entrusted us to use for the good of his kingdom and his purposes in the world.

But I can't let us forget those thrilling words. By using what we've been given to maximize kingdom purposes, we are given the opportunity to "enter into the joy" of our master. We feel it. We enjoy it. We share it with our master.

We revel in it and are inspired by it. We never want to live without it again, this joy that Jesus feels when his servants invest in his kingdom with what they've been given.

This is what changed me. In the story I'm about to tell you, I was doing good works, but I had not fully invested the things of great worth that God had given to me. I had not fully maximized what had been entrusted to me. When I finally did, it changed my life and the lives of nearly everyone I had an opportunity to impact afterward.

Now, remember that this book is about you. So let me ask you to start thinking about this question: What gifts of great value has God entrusted to you? Go back three paragraphs and think over that partial list I gave of what they might look like. Do you find yourself on this list? Are there other things you've been entrusted with? Ponder this as we continue through the pages. Trust me, this question—what has God given you for making a difference in the world?—is among the most important questions you'll ever answer about your life.

Chapter 2

A Journey to Joy

We make a living by what we get, but we make a life by what we give.

—Winston Churchill

The story of the talents that we just explored isn't just abstract spiritual truth to me. It isn't merely a passing Sunday school lesson. It is about something real. It has power. It has defined my life. Its meaning has become much of what I'm about, much of what I want to encourage in the world. Let me tell you my story so you can see up close a life transformed by these ancient words.

A few decades ago, I had the privilege of working for a wonderful organization called Walk Thru the Bible (WTB), which used innovative ways of teaching the Bible around the world. My background had been in sales, so when I went to work for WTB, I was initially in their publishing division. But shortly thereafter, I was set to the task of working with charitable families. Essentially, I was a caseload manager responsible for building relationships with the people who supported this valuable organization. I managed a portfolio of approximately one hundred relationships when I first started. I loved what I did. It fit my gifts, got me involved with people I respected, and allowed me to do good in the world. I was grateful for my role.

It was just as I was hitting my stride in this work that the founder of Walk Thru the Bible, Bruce Wilkinson, stepped in and changed my life. Now, you may know Bruce Wilkinson as the author of the phenomenally popular book *The Prayer of Jabez*, one of the most successful publications in the history of religious publishing. I knew him before this book came out. He is a gifted teacher, a statesman, and a wise leader. I am privileged to call him a friend.

Now, Bruce is also a powerful speaker, and it was during one of his speeches that he rocked my world! I remember that he was talking to a gathering of about a thousand pastors in Atlanta, and his topic was the Parable of the Talents. I had read that parable many times, but when Bruce taught, the rich meaning of it lit up for me.

I saw for the first time that in the Bible, a talent is not just money, nor does it mean what it does in English. Instead, the whole parable is about what God has given each human being, about the way he has made them so that they have gifts meant to be invested in his kingdom.

This was completely mind-blowing to me. I had never seen this before.

It changed me, as did the illustration Bruce gave along with his talk. Now, Bruce can be refreshingly blunt, and that day, he did something I will never forget. He was talking about the idea of increase and the obligation of all of us to expand the talents God has given us—using the word *talents*, of course, in the broad sense as it is used in the parable.

As he was speaking, he said, "Let me illustrate what I'm talking about," and he stepped up to a pastor sitting near the front of the room. Now, remember, this is in front of nearly a thousand other pastors. To this lone pastor, he said, "Tell me about you. How long have you been in your church? What was the size of the church when you came, and what's the size of the church today? Describe the impact of the church."

As you can imagine, this pastor was quaking in his boots! But there was no escape. He started describing his church and explaining that he had about eight hundred members.

Bruce then asked, "How long have you been at the church?"

"Fifteen years," the man said.

"And what was the attendance at the church when you started there?" Bruce asked.

"Well, about eight hundred," the pastor said, just beginning to realize what was coming.

Bruce then looked at this man kindly but purpose-fully and said, "OK, if the talent God gave you was that church, and you had eight hundred people when you got there, and you have eight hundred people today, what can you tell me you've done with that church that would show you've expanded the talents God has given you?"

Man, was there some squirming going on in that room! I felt for that poor man, but I also appreciated Bruce's bold-ness. He was trying to move all those pastors to a new level. He was trying to keep them from settling. And he was trying to bring the words of Jesus in the Parable of the Talents to bear upon all the lives in that room.

After this event, Bruce and I got in the car together, and he immediately said, "So what'd you think?"

Frankly, I was still recovering a bit, both from the impact of what God was doing in my heart and from the awkward moment with that pastor. Still, I knew a challenge when I met one, and I decided to be straight with Bruce about what was happening to me.

"Well," I said, "I'm not sure I'm qualified to comment on what happened between you and that pastor. But I'll tell you what happened in my heart while you were speaking."

"OK, go ahead," Bruce said with typical intensity.

I said, "Bruce, I realized as you spoke that I have been entrusted by God with a caseload of charitable givers. And Walk Thru the Bible has also entrusted me with these giv-ers. No one else is responsible for stewarding that group of donors besides me. So this is my talent, and I need to maximize it. I need to give God and WTB a great return. So I'm committing to getting my caseload up to a million dollars in five years."

Now, you need to know what Bruce knew. My portfolio of givers was contributing about five hundred thousand dollars a year at that time. In addition, I wasn't even the head of my department. So to think in terms of doubling that amount in five years was beyond bold. Still, I knew it was right. I remember saying to myself as Bruce spoke, "Bob, you need to double the talents that have been entrusted to you. You need to increase that base of giving to a million dollars."

Bruce was nothing but encouraging. In fact, I sensed that what I was saying was just the kind of impact he had hoped to make. I will be grateful for that moment in Atlanta, along with Bruce's encouragement and coaching, for the rest of my life.

The story of the talents lived in me after this. I thought about it constantly and put it into practice. And God honored his words. I had set a goal of increasing the yield from my caseload to a million dollars in five years. It didn't happen that way. Instead, it took only two and a half years!

You can imagine how thrilled I was. And trust me, I didn't think this was all about me. It was a humbling privilege to feel like I was serving God with what he had given me. I was also awed by what this increased giving meant for Walk Thru the Bible. It meant that we could expand our ministry. At that time, it meant specifically that we could go into Russia, a land just opening up to outside influence, and teach the Bible where it had long been forbidden. I was also moved by what I saw in the lives of our donors as they invested in the kingdom of God. It changed them in ways too marvelous to count.

I became a man set on fire by the truth of the talents. It helped that God kept adding to my understanding of this parable. I remember that some years later, I heard another man talk about Jesus's teaching on the talents. I'll never forget that he read the whole parable as he began. Of course, I had been such a student of this story since that day in Atlanta with Bruce that I knew the story well. I had practically memorized every word of what Jesus said.

Yet it was then that I heard it in a way that had never registered with me before. Though the speaker didn't read any of the words with special emphasis, it struck me powerfully that not only is the faithful man in the parable entrusted with a greater position than he had before, but he is also told he can enter into his master's joy.

Now, I had heard this parable a thousand times, but those words about entering into the joy of the master echoed in my heart as if for the first time. At that moment, God opened my eyes to a special relationship he was offering. He was calling me to intimacy. He seemed to be saying, "If you do what I made you for, invest what I have given you, you will draw so near to me that you will literally share my joy." As these words settled into me, I had a deep hunger to know the Lord and step into his joy. I wanted the relationship he was offering, the relationship of joy I was made for—that we are all made for!

This fresh understanding of that parable was transforming. I so wanted to please God and fulfill his purposes that it prompted some soul-piercing questions about how I lived out my calling. How was I treating the donors with whom I'd developed relationships? And what about my coworkers? Had I been a good and true friend to all? Did I genuinely care about them as individuals? Was I honest and forthright with them? Was my only goal to raise money, or was it also to love and care for the people God had brought into my life? These were heavy questions, and I took them to heart.

I made the needed changes, and as I did, beautiful things began to happen, things that lined up perfectly with the parable. The number of relationships that I found myself cultivating grew. Soon I was playing the part of friend and advisor as I got into other people's lives and truly cared. I felt like I was investing in people, not trying to coax them—drawing them out toward their purpose and calling, not just urging them to invest in mine.

The truth at the heart of the Parable of the Talents confirmed itself over and over again. During the next ten years, our pool of givers and ambassadors at Walk Thru the Bible grew from several dozen to more than 1,400. Meanwhile, our contribution revenue climbed to $10.5 million. Our sustained growth was at an unprecedented 30 to 35 percent in my final five years.

Personally, I was enjoying incomparable affirmation from the board and leadership at WTB and from donor families, peers, and staff. In a way, I felt like I was hearing, "Well done, good and faithful servant."

Along with our growth as an organization, my role and responsibilities increased. I managed special projects. My borders were bulging. I felt as if God was saying, "You were faithful with a few things, I will put you in charge of many things."

And I was so fulfilled! I was happy and motivated, excited and enthusiastic. At the time, I was operating in the sweet spot of my calling. The team at WTB felt God smiling as he said, "Enter into my joy!"

Friends and colleagues were noticing the work I was doing and began to challenge me. One in particular encouraged me to share my knowledge and experience with other organizations so they could perhaps realize the same type of growth, ultimately expanding the kingdom of God.

With approval from the leadership at WTB, I began investing small segments of time with Moody Bible Institute, teaching them how to open their doors to new donors, ambassadors, and supporters. We designed a similar strategy at Moody as we had at WTB. Implementing the first phase, we showcased the work of Moody to see if donors would respond, and boy, did they! Eventually, Moody would attribute $20 million in cash gifts, another more than $20 million in deferred and planned giving, and dozens upon dozens of new donors to the work we did together.

Talk about pure joy and a spiritual high! I was cruising!

But wait a second. You know as well as I do that life is not always smooth sailing; our boats get rocked at times. Mine was about to.

Why?

Because God had *more* for me. And he had more for those whose lives and ministries I could touch with the gifts he'd given me.

Little did I realize at the time, but in order to invest *all* the talents God had given me, I would need blind faith and unfathomable courage. Faith to step out and go where I'd never ventured before. Faith to say, "OK, Lord, I feel you leading me to take this giant leap—and I'm trusting you to help me fly!"

That's the kind of faith I needed after having a heart-to-heart with my friend Chris Crane, who at the time was the CEO of one of the largest Christian microfinance companies in the world. I remember that he asked me, "Bob, what would be a better use of your gifts? Investing all of them in one organization, or investing them in multiple organizations?"

As we continued to talk, Chris forced me to consider my real God-given talent. To him, it was a no-brainer that I was designed to team up with several organizations to develop powerful growth strategies.

That's when the lights came on. Suddenly, I knew God wanted me to leverage the gifts he'd given me and multiply them exponentially to achieve an even more significant return for my master! Was it a risk? Yes! I had four children, a daughter about to start college, and very little money in the bank.

But I had no choice. God's purposes were increasingly clear to me. I couldn't imagine facing God at the finish line and having to confess, "Master, I was afraid to take the risk and leverage the talents you gave me. So I played it safe and stayed within the comfort zone of that one organization. I'm sorry, Lord. The pay was good, the benefits were solid, and I was in a comfortable routine."

Do you remember what the Parable of the Talents says about the servant who was given one talent, was afraid, and chose not to invest it? Here is what the parable tells us: "But his master answered him, 'You wicked and slothful servant! You knew that I reap where I have not sown and gather where I scattered no seed? Then you ought to have invested my money with the bankers, and at my coming I should have received what was my own with interest. So take the talent from him and give it to him who has the ten talents'" (Matt. 25:26–28).

So you see, I *had to* venture out into the unknown.

Adding to the drama of this moment was the fact that I was going through one of the worst times in my life, as I've mentioned. It would be inappropriate for me to go into too much detail, but I don't want to soften the pain of those days. I want you to be able to see clearly how God sometimes works. To state it briefly, my family was going through a swirling, bruising season. We were all traumatized. We were all hurting. I tended all this to the best of my ability, yet I also knew that I was at a crossroads in my calling, and I needed to be obedient to God.

It was clear as it could be that God was calling me to start a firm that would put my talents to greater use. This is when Westfall Group, now known as Westfall Gold, was born.

It is easy to write these words today. The reality at the time was more daunting. Some of this was for wonderful reasons. For example, it was just as I was launching Westfall Group that I was offered an amazing job, a role that I would have seen as nearly the purpose of my life only a few months before. Yet, certain of what I was meant to do, I turned it down. Keep in mind that I was only forty-one years old in 2002 when this happened. That's not an age when most men are turning down life-changing jobs. And sure, I definitely had to battle some uncertainty. Each time, though, I quickly came back to confidence in my decision.

The offers didn't end there. At about the same time, the Billy Graham Evangelistic Association called and asked me to be the chief of fund-raising for the new Billy Graham Center. They made it clear that if I was successful in that role, it could eventually lead to me being the chief of development for their entire organization. Now, you need to know that I came to faith through the ministry of Billy Graham. So the idea of working for that revered ministry was beyond anything I'd ever dreamed. Still, I had to turn them down too. I was certain of the direction God had for me, and it wouldn't have been good for them or me to deviate from God's purposes.

Some of the other factors making that season challenging were less complimentary. There were the family troubles I've already mentioned. Then there were the natural doubts and disappointments of some of the people around me. And of course, whenever you step out in a new direction based on faith and courage alone, you have doubts and concerns of your own. This was certainly true of me at the time, even as determined as I was to do the will of God.

I say these things not to impress you with my hardships but to make sure I tell you the truth. I don't want to sugarcoat my story so that you are surprised when you take your own steps of faith and deal with some struggles. Hard things happen—for all of us. They are a part of life in this world. Hear me, please. You have to face them down. You have to stand your ground. You have to insist on investing what has been entrusted to you no matter the opposition. Too much good is in the balance. Too many people are waiting for the impact you can have.

Now, here is the rest of the Westfall Group story. We started with two clients and a vision to help three to five organizations raise a total of $15 million in five years. Over time, we created some innovative strategies, one of which was our unique Donor Weekend, in which generous givers are "brought into the family," helped to understand the vision of an organization, and given an opportunity to contribute in a relational and meaningful way. It has proven stunningly successful through the years, and I am grateful for the great good it has meant for organizations devoted to making a difference.

It did not take long for more clients to come our way. As I've mentioned already, among our first was Moody Bible Institute—an early adopter of our Donor Weekend approach. Soon Youth with a Mission San Diego / Baja contacted me, also eager to work with us on Donor Weekends. After this, famed evangelist Luis Palau called. Our work with his firm produced grand results, as did our work with Asbury Seminary and Knox Area Rescue Ministries and too many other organizations through the years to mention here.

Rather than tell you detailed stories from our history, I would rather let the heroes I'm about to describe reveal the truths we encourage people and leading organizations to live out. Yet let me tell you one very strong memory I have from our history, since I think it will be an encouragement to you.

We were working with a major organization in 2008. I remember that we started, as usual, on Thursday night. On Friday, the stock market underwent the worst crash since the Great Depression. I'm sure you remember that moment. Our team looked at each other and said, "Oh my, this is going to be bad. This is going to be a total failure." We assumed that people would not want to give at that event for fear of what was happening in the country.

Yet the reverse happened. The donors that weekend gave a huge amount. It was as though they had confidence in the Parable of the Talents when they didn't have that much confidence in the American stock market. And they gave. They invested. They fulfilled the will of their God and entered into the joy of their master. It was a sight to see, and I have seen moments like it many times since.

Here is what I want you to know. As I write these words late in 2019, Westfall Gold has just reached our goal of raising $1 billion for the organizations it serves. Yes! A billion! I don't possess the words to tell you what this means to me. Remember that I was originally hoping to help up to five organizations raise perhaps $15 million. And that was a distant dream at the time. Now we've reached a billion dollars. In fact, by the time you read these words, we will be well past that milestone.

My team members now wonder aloud about when

we might reach $5 billion or even $10 billion. This isn't arrogance. It is a combination of seasoned faith in God, confidence in the truth and promises of the Parable of the Talents, and certainty that most people are eager to invest in God's kingdom when they are given effective ways to do it.

Now, I've spoken a lot about money here. I don't want you to get the wrong impression. My business is helping good organizations raise money. So I report growth and kingdom principles in financial terms. If my firm made bricks or shoes or cars or houses, I would talk to you in those terms. I work with money given to causes that do great good in the world.

Yet I don't want my descriptions of my work to distract from what you might be called to do. All I have done is live out the Parable of the Talents. All I have done is taken God at his word, summoned the courage, defied the opposition, and invested what I was given to invest. That's why I have a story to tell you now.

Here are my questions for you: What is your story? What is your gift? What is your investment? The point of this book isn't to tell you Bob Westfall's story. It is for you to write the story you are meant to write. So take some time. Perhaps you should set this book aside for a few hours and think through what God has given you. What is your talent of silver? What does he want you to maximize? What is your kingdom work?

That's the heart of the matter. My story is already being written. It may be time for yours to begin or for you to write some grand new chapters in the story you've already begun.

Whatever the case, I want the tales I'm about to tell in the pages that follow to help you, to ignite fires in you, and to move you to live out the great adventure you are made for.

Chapter 3

What's That in Your Hand?

Work while you have light. You are responsible for the talent that has been entrusted to you.

—Henri Frédéric Amiel

S o far in this book, I've been speaking to you in fairly vast terms. I've taken the Parable of the Talents and added the historical facts that force us to think in terms of hundreds of pounds of silver and decades of a man's labor. I've told my own story, referring to large organizations and goals that reach to the billions of dollars. Your mind may be reeling a bit. I would certainly understand if it were.

Yet it is important for us not to miss a truth here. The calling of God on us all to invest our talents, to put what we've been given in play for the good of people and the advancement of God's kingdom, applies to every stage of life and every level of sophistication. It applies to the simple and the complex, to the visible and the largely unseen, to the vital things of life and the seemingly unimportant.

Let me tell you a story that I trust will bring this home for you. Years ago, a well-known pastor friend knew I was traveling to the Dallas–Fort Worth area and asked if I would meet with his son, a seminary student there. "He's really down right now," my friend said. "He needs some advice and encouragement. And he respects you."

I agreed and set up a time to meet.

After small talk over breakfast, I said to the young man, "Tell me how it's going."

"Terrible. Just awful," the young man said. "Here I am, a seminary student, and I feel like God has called me to be the senior pastor of a church. I'm so frustrated. I know I'm supposed to be a senior pastor."

"Hold on a second," I said. "You're still in school. You're working toward your degree. I'm sure God still has some things he wants to show you."

The young man wrung his hands and moved uncomfortably in his chair. No, he was ready to pastor. It was straight to the top for him.

"Tell me, what are you doing today, besides school?" I asked.

"I've got to help pay for seminary, so I cut grass. I've formed a small landscaping company. Two guys work for me."

"Oh? Tell me the spiritual condition of the two guys who work for you."

He squinted. "I have no idea . . . I mean, we cut grass."

"OK, tell me what you're doing in church."

"Well, I'm an associate pastor, and I teach a Sunday school class."

"How many people are in the class?"

"Just two couples right now."

"And what's the spiritual condition of those two couples?"

He ran a hand through his hair and shook his head. "I really don't think they're that spiritual. They're not committed. A lot of times, they don't show up. It's been a real battle—like pulling teeth!"

I knew what was happening. As an outsider, it was clear as day to me. But he couldn't see it. Perhaps he didn't want to.

"What I'd like you to do is take a look at the Parable of the Talents," I said, "and imagine for a moment that you have two talents God has entrusted to you: the couples in your Sunday school class and the workers in your landscape business."

He stared at me blankly.

"Now I'm going to ask you what the master asks the servants in the parable: 'I've entrusted two talents to you. What have you done with them?'"

I'm telling you, I watched the blood drain from the young man's face.

Silence fell over our table.

"Nothing," was all he could muster.

God's Word had found its way to the core of his being.

"Remember the promise?" I asked. "Once the servant said, 'Master, you entrusted to me two talents; see, I have gained two more talents.' His master said to him, 'Well done, good and faithful servant.' Of course, everybody wants to hear those words. But let's think about what the master says next: 'You were faithful with a few things, I will put you in charge of many things; enter into the joy of your master.'

"What your actions say to me is that the two guys who work for you and the two couples in your Sunday school class are not important to you," I said. "What's important to you is *your dream* to be a senior pastor. But what God wants you to do is not forsake the two talents he's given you. In other words, the end does not justify the means."

I've seen this scenario a million times. A pastor wants a megaministry or a global outreach. He's gone days on end, slaving away at his dream, up late and out early. Meanwhile, his wife and children are at home, wilting from his neglect.

"What God's looking for," I told the young man, "is faithfulness in the little things, the things that may not seem important to you. Are you going to invest in what God has given you today, the things you may not have even noticed, but the things that, I can assure you, matter to him? When you show that you value the talents he's already given you, *then* he can trust you with more—and you can enter into his joy."

I could tell that what I said impacted him, and I hoped that the conviction and determination I saw in his face would remain with him and bring change. You know how it is. We can never be sure how our words impact someone after they have left us.

Yet that evening, my friend, the young man's father, phoned me.

"What did you do to my son?"

"Only what we talked about," I said. "I gave him some advice and encouraged him."

"Well, he listened to you!"

I was grateful to hear it. I've also been grateful through the years since to watch that young man's rise. He obviously did what I told him to do. He started investing. He started prioritizing God's priorities. He started maximizing the talents God had given him. Today, he is a highly respected speaker and leader. It has all been due to his hard work and God's grace, but I'm grateful I had the opportunity to be there when he was down, when he needed his vision refocused and his priorities realigned. God knows I've often needed this in my own life.

Time and again in the Bible, God asks people what they have in their hands. In other words, what do you have that you can invest, what are the things you already possess that God wants to use? In short, what has God already given you?

Moses was asked what was in his hand. He carried only a staff. Not only did God use that staff to confirm his calling on Moses's life (by turning that staff into a snake—yikes!), but Moses would ultimately use that staff in leading his people to the promised land.

A young boy who was following Jesus around Israel only had a few loaves of bread and some fish in his hand. When he offered them to Jesus, those few loaves and fish were multiplied to feed thousands of people. That little boy's generosity became the basis of a miracle of increase that people the world over still talk about to this day.

You see my point. The Parable of the Talents applies to frustrated seminary students and men wandering in the wilderness and little boys who have only what seems insignificant to give. And God uses it all. But he does so only after someone has the courage to invest what they have.

And what about you? You are going to hear me ask this again and again in these pages. This book is about you. You are meant to be the hero of the story. So here is the all-important question: What is in your hand? What is the talent, the gift, the thing entrusted to you that you are meant to maximize, to increase, to see grow for the good of others because you had the courage to invest it? It may seem unimportant. Or it may seem huge. Either way, invest what you have. Trust God. Watch the increase come. Thrill at what the good God will accomplish in the world with what you have given him.

And joy will come as you do.

Chapter 4

In the Direction of Hope

A really great talent finds its happiness in execution.

—Johann Wolfgang von Goethe

I t was a beautiful spring day in 2018, and Southwest Airlines flight 1380 was streaking through the skies from New York to Dallas. In charge was Captain Tammie Jo Shults. Though the passengers aboard the plane that day could not have known it, they were in exceptional hands.

Captain Shults was not just any pilot. She had been a pioneering naval aviator who was one of the first women ever to qualify in the F/A-18 Hornet. She served as an instructor for naval aviators during Operation Desert Storm in Iraq, since the U.S. combat exclusion policy kept females from flying combat missions. So she trained the men who did. She rose to the rank of lieutenant commander, was decorated many times for her skills and excellence, and eventually left the navy to the great regret of those who had served with her.

She then began flying for Southwest Airlines, but only part-time. She wanted to do a similarly excellent job raising the family she had started with her husband, fellow naval aviator Dean Shults.

All this brought her to this day, April 17, 2018. As her Boeing 737 sped toward Dallas, an engine fan blade suddenly failed, sending debris into the left side of the fuselage and one side window. The window blew out, causing the plane to decompress. A woman sitting next to the window was partially pulled out of the plane, which caused her death.

It was then that all of Captain Shults's training and experience shone. She remained amazingly calm. She immediately determined two things: First, the plane would not crash but instead make a successful landing. Second, she would land the plane in Philadelphia.

You have to picture this scene. One engine has failed. There is a hole in the fuselage. The cabin has decompressed, which means objects are swirling through the air inside the plane. The oxygen masks have dropped, helping people breathe but also confirming that something is tragically wrong and that a crash might be imminent. The noise is deafening.

Maintaining command, Captain Shults passed the message to her crew: they were going to land in Philadelphia, and they weren't going to crash. Because of the noise and failing systems, this message was then passed row by row to all the passengers.

And she did it. She made an emergency descent and landed in Philadelphia. She showed such calm and competence that legendary Captain Chesley Sullenberger, pilot of the famed U.S. Airways flight 1549 that landed on the Hudson River in 2009 with all passengers surviving, commended her astonishing performance.

By the way, she was not supposed to be flying that day. She had swapped shifts with the pilot who was scheduled for that flight—her husband, Dean Shults!

She was celebrated widely and even honored by Congress. But this is what I want you to know about Captain Shults: she is also a devout Christian. When she was speaking about her experience in a church one Sunday, she said, "When you have a destination, you have hope. *And hope changes everything.*"

For decades, I've been working with people as they invested their gifts to achieve grand things. I can tell you that hope is always at the heart of these decisions. Hope born of a clear direction. A person commits something of value to achieve a noble end. This gives them new direction. And hope rises. Then there is the good this generosity does in the lives of the hurting and needy. Provision comes. Care is provided. And hope rises. There is also what happens when others hear about it. They learn of an ambitious plan for doing good. Perhaps they join in. They are changed by the experience. And hope rises in their own hearts. Hope then reproduces itself, perhaps millions of times.

It is all because of the truth expounded by that great prophet, Captain Tammie Jo Shults! "When you have a destination, you have hope. *And hope changes everything.*"

This always brings me back to the Parable of the Talents. You see, the servant who was entrusted with one talent had no hope. He had fear. He did not expect that he could expand and increase what he'd been given, so he buried it in a hole. The future was his enemy, not a promise. So he merely worked to dodge danger, not to invest for impact. He was condemned then, and his one talent was taken away from him and given to those more deserving.

The other two servants, the one with five talents and the one with two, defied whatever fear they might have been feeling and chose instead to see the future as a field of promise. They invested. In other words, they maximized; they grew. They did what you do when you want increase. They lived in hope. They had direction. So they were promoted, given more responsibility, and given the talent of the man who gave in to his fear.

"Daddy, Will You Build Another?"

When I think of this dynamic of hope, I think of Sean Lambert, the founder and president of Youth with a Mission (YWAM) San Diego / Baja. YWAM is a large international, interdenominational movement started in 1960 by Loren Cunningham with the goal of knowing God and making him known. YWAM San Diego / Baja is a founding client of Westfall Gold—and a fond client too! We love them and admire what they do.

While on a mission trip to Tijuana, Mexico, in May of 1990, Sean and his daughter, Andrea, joined a team of fifteen people to build a house for a poverty-stricken family. When the house was completed and the family moved in, Andrea pointed out another poor family living in an old abandoned bus adjacent to the new "home of hope" being built. She said, "Daddy, are you going to build a house for that family too? What about the family living in the bus? Are you going to build them a house?"

Andrea's words moved Sean to build a second house and to come up with a plan for more still. And Homes of Hope was born. Starting with this single house in Tijuana, Mexico, Homes of Hope has now built 6,300 homes for poor families in twenty-three nations. Amazingly, they have also involved more than 130,000 volunteers in their projects. One of the "talents" knitted into Sean's makeup is his love and compassion for the poor. He was faithful to the one house God sent him to build, and so God put him in charge of many. Today, Homes of Hope impacts poor families economically and spiritually, through education, and in terms of social/emotional health too.

Sean is an excellent example of someone who took small, simple steps in obeying God. He entered into all God wanted to do through his life in a ministry that is now impacting ten other nations . . . and growing!

Think of the hope factor in what Sean has done. He is guided by hope as he pursues a vision. He gives hope to those who will live in the houses that Homes of Hope builds. And think of what is happening in the hearts of those 130,000 volunteers. And those who hear about Homes of Hope. Do you see what is happening? As Captain Shults said, direction gives hope, and hope changes everything.

Free Wheelchair Mission

This hope factor also makes me think of Don Schoendorfer. Over thirty years ago, he watched a disabled woman drag herself across a dirt road in Morocco. The mental image of her anguish and loss of dignity haunted him for years after. Finally, in 1999, Don gave in to God's prompting to do something about it.

You see, Don not only had recurring thoughts about the handicapped Moroccan woman and a desire to help the millions of people who can't walk; he also had a PhD in mechanical engineering. So he created a simple, rugged, inexpensive wheelchair made of a plastic lawn chair, a steel frame, and a pair of bicycle tires.

When Don realized his design could be built and shipped for under sixty dollars each, Free Wheelchair Mission was born. Since then, the ministry has provided nearly 1.2 million wheelchairs, offering hope and dignity to people with disabilities in ninety-three countries, including some in South America, Africa, Latin America and the Caribbean, Eastern Europe, the Middle East, Asia, and the Pacific.

Did you get that? Nearly 1.2 million wheelchairs. Do you see it? "You were faithful with a few things; I will put you in charge of many things."

A volunteer for Free Wheelchair Mission, Ines Franklin, says, "When one of our recipients gets seated in that chair for the first time, it's magical." Another volunteer says, "When you lift somebody off the ground, it by far overshadows any other experience."

When you hear these words, does the summons to "enter into the joy of your master" come to mind? I can just see the Lord smiling when Don and his team seat someone in one of those wheelchairs, someone who's been crawling their entire life, and say, "This wheelchair is for you. We want you to feel like you are resting in God's hands when you sit in it." I don't know about you, but to me, *that* is ministry. To me, *that* is true religion. It's life abundant, which is what Christ calls us to. It's pure joy!

And get this. The goal of Free Wheelchair Mission is to provide *twenty million* wheelchairs to those in need. "These people are on the ground now, waiting," says Don. "They're waiting for us to provide a wheelchair. We don't want to take a hundred years to solve this problem. There's no reason why we can't begin to solve it now."

Who gave Don his ability? Who allowed him to see that Moroccan woman? Who put the desire in his heart to do something? God did. And Don was obedient. He didn't get caught up worrying that he was only one man with a strange and radical idea in his head. He moved forward, one step at a time.

There was grunt work involved. It wasn't easy. There was no promise his idea would succeed. But with God driving the plan, Don could not fail. And neither could Free Wheelchair Mission. And hope rises in the hearts and in the lands Free Wheelchair Mission touches—in Don's heart perhaps most of all!

Grief, Genius, and Generosity

Sometimes, hope rises from seeming hopelessness. Let me tell you about another man who was a mechanical engineer—and who, when tragedy struck his life, turned out to be a lifesaver. His name is Parker H. "Pete" Petit, and the home medical monitor he invented saved my daughter Jessica's life!

It was the summer of 1970. Up to that point, everything was going "as planned." Pete had earned his bachelor's and master's degrees in mechanical engineering from the Georgia Institute of Technology and had a promising job as a project manager at Lockheed in Marietta, Georgia. Just then, however, Pete's infant son Brett died in his crib. Overnight, Pete and his wife joined the thousands of parents whose children had lost their lives in crib deaths to sudden infant death syndrome (SIDS).

As Pete and his wife mourned and tried to keep going, questions plagued Pete about why this had happened and if it could have been prevented. He soon learned that deaths similar to Brett's were being avoided, but only in hospitals where expensive monitoring units were available to prevent them.

Pete had an idea. What if someone were to create and develop a smaller, portable monitoring unit that people could rent and have in their homes when their children were at risk for SIDS? And what if that someone was Pete?

From that moment on, Pete poured everything he had into his new lifesaving creation. He resigned from his job at Lockheed in early 1971 and took night classes to earn his MBA at Georgia State University, where he learned more about business and finance. While he was taking classes, he raised funding and founded a company that would later become Healthdyne, Inc., a manufacturer of high-tech health-care devices and provider of health-care information systems, technology, health-care services, and disease management tactics.

Pete had a plan for his life, but the death of his son redirected it. He took his grief and turned it into a passion for saving lives by creating an affordable, take-home respiratory and heart monitor that keeps watch over ten thousand infants a year. This monitor has saved tens of thousands of lives, including that of my now thirty-year-old daughter, Jessica, who was monitored as an infant when her life was threatened by SIDS.

But Pete didn't stop there. Far from it. In order to increase shareholder value, Healthdyne was split into three publicly traded companies whose annual revenues grew in excess of $1 billion in 1996. Pete has served on the board of directors and board of trustees for major corporations and organizations, including Atlantic Southeast Airlines, Intelligent Systems, and the National Health Museum. He has donated millions of dollars to a variety of worthy philanthropy projects.

Often in the stories of investment that I'm privileged to know, tragedy causes hope to dim. Then a destination makes itself known. Someone courageously begins to invest, and hope rises—often for millions of people.

The Courage to CURE

Finally, let me tell you the amazing story of my friend and former client Dr. Scott Harrison. He was an orthopedic surgeon with a thriving practice in the United States when he was invited by another surgeon to travel to Malawi, Africa, to perform and teach spinal surgery.

Initially, Dr. Harrison determined he would make one trip and that would be the end of it. Yet performing intricate, interesting procedures that were curing spinal deformities in a developing nation was much more rewarding than he ever imagined. Dr. Harrison found himself returning to Africa again and again, often for months at a time.

Eventually, he was asked to become the CEO of a large New York Stock Exchange company that was failing. At first, he was uninterested. Though he was gifted in business, it didn't seem like something God wanted him to do. Yet as he and his wife, Sally, began praying, it became clear to Dr. Harrison that he was supposed to take the job. He says it was one of the times in his life when he received a clear answer to prayer. It seemed strange at the time, and it confused him, but he was obedient and left his practice of twenty years to enter the corporate world. In the years that followed, he helped turn the company around, sold it in a merger, and was once again free to pursue his passion.

It didn't take Dr. Harrison long to return to Africa to continue helping the less fortunate. He also began searching for an agency he could work with in Africa—but he found none. Sally and Scott took this as a commission. They would have to make it happen. God's leading was clear. Using Scott's extensive business experience and surgical skills, he and Sally set out to found CURE International.

Talk about dreaming big! When Scott and Sally were first planning CURE, they drew directly from Jesus's example in the Scriptures when he sent out the twelve and later the seventy-two to minister, instructing them to do two things: heal the sick and preach the gospel. This was important to the Harrisons because they knew that most of the U.S. agencies that existed to help cure diseases overseas had at most a 5 percent focus on the gospel. Most organizations had no emphasis on faith at all. Often, these organizations were about the surgeons more than the patients.

On another trip to Africa, this time to Kenya, Dr. Harrison met a missionary who had a similar passion. Their hearts and purposes became intertwined. Together, they opened their first hospital. That was in 1998. Today, CURE International has a presence in more than fourteen countries. They have performed 213,800 procedures and treated more than three million patients. As important, they have presented the gospel of Jesus to more than a million people since CURE began.

If that doesn't give you chills, I don't know what will! And Scott and Sally have held steadfast to their plan and unique vision for CURE, which is to bring physical and spiritual healing to children with disabilities in the developing world. As I write this, CURE is transforming the lives of children with hydrocephalus, cleft lip and palate, spine deformities, clubfoot, and other crippling orthopedic conditions. In fact, more than 126,600 children have been treated at CURE clubfoot partner clinics, and fifteen thousand procedures have been performed to treat hydrocephalus and spina bifida. These children and their families often feel great shame and face rejection from their relatives and communities, but at CURE, they find acceptance and hope as hospital staff members express God's love for them.

Remarkably, Scott is convinced that if he had not followed God's guidance to make the leap into corporate leadership years earlier, using a gift he knew he had but was unsure how to use, he would still be working in his medical practice.

God gives us the freedom to say no to his dynamic plans. He'll let us live easily and anonymously in service to him—but it often won't be his best. We often won't be all we can be. It won't be ultimately fulfilling.

There is a smaller tale within this broader CURE story that always moves me. When we first began to approach CURE with our model, we could tell their board was a bit skeptical. You see, our trademark Donor Weekend is oriented toward ministry to and the edification of those who attend. It is intended, as I told CURE at the time, to be "a gift to your donors." There are devotionals and keynote speakers and opportunities for fellowship and worship that are deeply meaningful. Even when we work with secular organizations, we still keep a focus on edification and the personal lives of leaders. It is all a very nontraditional approach. But frankly, that is why it works so well.

Fortunately, CURE's senior vice president for marketing at the time we started working with them was a stellar woman named Lisa Wolf. As she explains, it was this ministry approach to a Donor Weekend that the CURE board was "skeptical about at first. Because in traditional fund-raising, you're all about making the ask. The idea of community building—and building trust—wasn't there yet. It was a different mind-set."

Still, we were asking CURE to step out and use their talents. Lisa did the same. She stepped out and became our champion, and thankfully, CURE became our client. Yet Lisa was still taking a risk. As she later told us, some of the board members approached her and said, "This event is not going to work." They felt like their organization had spent months preparing, but people weren't going to come. The whole event would be a failure.

Our champion was feeling the pressure. The doubts around her were getting to her, and she was, as she later told us, terrified: "First, I'm wondering if we had made a mistake believing in this fund-raising model. Plus, I'll be blamed if this thing tanks. What do we do if it fails? And in the back of my mind, I was taunted by the idea it might fail."

Once the event began, though, something marvelous happened. Dr. Harrison approached Lisa halfway through the weekend and said, "You know what? If this doesn't raise a dime, it will have been worth it."

Lisa responded, "Well, Scott, we're going to raise a lot more than a dime!" But she was touched by his change of heart. "Scott is a deeply faithful man," she told me later. "When he saw the Bible teaching, the worship music, and the sense of community that was already developing among the attendees, he was sold."

That first weekend was a success, as were the many events we did with CURE afterward. Yet what I want you to see is how courage builds on courage, how boldness summons boldness. We had to be bold to believe in our model. Lisa had to be courageous to stand for what she knew would work—despite the doubts that hounded her. CURE had to be willing to step out and trust God, us, and Lisa. The courage and faith of all of us had to be put into play in the lives of the donors who gathered that weekend. And God hovered over it all, fulfilling his promises.

Yet what I want you to focus on most is the hope factor in Scott Harrison's life. He went on that first trip to Malawi. He served people with medical care. New direction came to him, as it did for his patients. Hope arose and changed everything. He kept going back. He became a CEO. The dream percolated in his soul while he was a corporate leader. New direction. More vision. More hope.

Then finally, CURE was born. It changed lives—the Harrisons' and their team's, as well as those of the many volunteers and of course the millions who were transformed by the message of Jesus and the dramatic effects of top-quality medical care. New direction. New hope. And everything is changed.

You know where I am going with this. I want you to apply Captain Shults's message to your life: "When you have a destination, you have hope. *And hope changes everything.*"

You have skills. You have some degree of wealth. You have experience and connections and other things of value. So what is your direction? What is the purpose of God for your life, for your talent and treasure? Where are you meant to go? Once you find the courage to do what you are meant to do, you will have new direction that leads to hope. And hope makes all the difference in your life and in the lives of others.

Thank you, Captain Shults. May we lead lives that are as courageous as you were on that April day!

Chapter 5

How the Vision Comes

People of talent resemble a musical instrument more closely than they do a musician. Without outside help, they produce not a single sound, but given even the slightest touch, and a magnificent tune emanates from them.

—Franz Grillparzer

We use the word *vision* in a variety of ways. There is the simple vision of seeing with our eyes, of course. Then there is the big vision some people get—a big picture from God or from skilled imagination that will define the rest of their lives.

Yet there is another kind of vision that relates to what we are talking about here. It is the vision that causes us to see a bit of what can happen if we invest what we have. It is the kind of vision that causes us to see familiar things in a new light, to perceive the value of what can happen if we courageously invest for a higher good.

One of our beloved clients at Westfall Gold is an organization called Mercy Ships. Its founder, Don Stephens, has one of the most inspiring stories of vision arising and investment happening that I know of. I want you to know that story, and I want you to see yourself in its meaning.

The vision that eventually shaped Don's life came to him when he was just nineteen years old. It seems he was on a mission trip to the Caribbean with a group of fellow Christians. They were serving the people in that region when they were forced into a bunker to wait out a powerful hurricane. As the winds began to die down, Don's group started surveying the horrible damage. It was just at that moment that a young woman said wistfully, "Wouldn't it be wonderful if there was a ship full of doctors and nurses that could come here at a time like this?"

As sometimes happens in life, those words landed almost fully formed in Don's heart and mind. He could see it: a huge ship equipped with surgical theaters and recovery wards, staffed by skilled doctors and nurses. It would be a portable hospital bringing transformative care to millions and millions of people.

Though he was only nineteen, that vision embedded itself in Don and would not leave him. It almost made no sense that he would be the one to have it. He was a tough kid from Colorado whose people were farmers and ranchers.

He knew nothing about ships and less about medical care. Yet it was as though the vision had chosen him.

Now, you might expect me to tell you that Don immediately began to see this vision become a reality. He didn't. Instead, time went by. Don served God in other ways. Then when he was in his early thirties, he had a chance to meet Mother Teresa. That meeting would focus the vision that eventually defined his life.

He was working for a Christian ministry in those days and was invited to visit the Sisters of Charity in India to explore ways to care for the disabled and the dying. Arrangements were also made for Don to meet Mother Teresa.

He was understandably excited to have time with such a legendary woman. To prepare, he filled notecards with the questions he would ask. He never got to use them, though. When he finally met Mother Teresa, it was her questions that guided their time together, not his.

With her typical directness, Mother Teresa asked three questions that changed Don's life. First, she asked, "What is your purpose? Why were you born?" Somewhat sheepishly, Don told her about the dream he had been carrying since he was nineteen. He knew how it must have sounded for someone like him to carry such a vast vision for so many years.

Don later said that it was at that moment Mother Teresa gave him a gift. She did not laugh. She did not dismiss. She was, in Don's words, "careful not to crush what was then a fragile, cherished hope." She listened. She encouraged. She was loving. In short, she honored Don's vulnerability.

Then she asked something that might have been searing and intrusive from the lips of another person. "Where is your pain?" she probed gently. "God often works through our pain to prepare us for our purpose."

Don remembers thinking that God had given Mother Teresa supernatural insight. The truth was that Don had been wrestling with tremendous pain at that time. He and his wife had only recently had their third child, John Paul, who was born severely disabled. Doctors had explained that the boy would never talk, and he would never feed or bathe himself. Don's agony was still fresh when Mother Teresa spoke what he took to be "very prophetic words."

She said, "Your son will help you on your journey to becoming the eyes, ears, mouth, and hands for the poor."

The words would hover over Don's life from that moment on. John Paul needed constant care every day—support groups, medicines, therapies, day care, education—and fortunately, Don lived in a country where these things were available. Yet millions of people, particularly in Africa, had no such care. The disabled were marginalized, however inadvertently, and left on the roadside of society. The care Don and his wife gave to John Paul increased their understanding of what millions in this world endure. It would be just as Mother Teresa said. John Paul helped Don and his wife on their journey.

Yet she wasn't done with her questions that day. Her final one put its finger on the critical point in Don's life: "What are you doing about your dream?" she asked.

The assumption of her question was clear. Most people never do anything about their dreams if they even dare to have them. Yet in playing it safe, in drawing back in fear, we deprive the world of what it so urgently needs. We also preclude the opportunity for what we give to be increased, to be expanded for noble purposes. Mother Teresa challenged Don to fulfill what was clearly his purpose—even if it seemed absolutely crazy!

Don left his time with the Sisters of Charity certain that he had to courageously take the steps toward doing what God had given him to do. He began looking for open doors. He started talking widely about using ships as hospitals to help the poor. He started making connections. Soon, others began to respond. Don says he would like to boast of his "fearless confidence," but what he actually had was "naïve confidence." Still, he stayed faithful. He put his talents into play.

Forty years have passed since that day with Mother Teresa. In those years, Mercy Ships has come into being, and it has had as many as four ships at a time making a difference in the world. It has not been easy. The first ship acquired was in such bad shape that they bought it as scrap metal. It took four years to refashion the ship to be ready for service. There have been sacrifices for Don and his family as well. They have found themselves living onboard one of the Mercy Ships for as long as a decade, serving and tending the needs of people.

I don't want anything about the Mercy Ships story to seem automatic. The dream Don received when he was nineteen required millions and millions of dollars to make a reality. It required the gifts and cooperation of thousands of people. As you can imagine, operating huge ships, hospitals, and all the crew and staff needed is spectacularly expensive and complicated. There have been challenges on top of challenges throughout the years.

Now let me tell you some good news. Mercy Ships has provided free surgeries and medical care to more than two million people in some seventy countries. Clinics have been established. Entire families and tribes have been transformed. As exciting, while these words are being written, Mercy Ships is just now finishing its first purpose-built hospital ship. The *Global Mercy* is bigger than any of the organization's previous ships and will have aboard not one but two hospitals with which to serve the poor and disabled. This first-ever ship will cost $126.5 million.

I don't share this cost to impress you with what people can do. I share it to impress you with what God will do when we invest our talents. In fact, this is what Don is impressed with as he looks back over Mercy Ships' forty-year journey. He recently said this to our team when we asked him what has surprised him the most about his adventure:

I'm in awe of this promise-keeping God. I'm in awe of that which was a seed thought, a dream in a boy's heart—a boy who was a son of the soil, a long way from the ocean, not knowing medicine or hospitals. But with a dream from God—and to see the reality of that is a huge and wonderful surprise. It makes me worship day in and day out, worship and give thanks to a God who is a promise-keeping God.

I can't tell you how inspired I am by Don Stephens and Mercy Ships. I am also deeply grateful that my firm has been privileged to work with them in raising the funds they need to touch so many lives.

Yet what inspires me most is what inspires Don. It is God. It is the way he takes what we give, what we invest, and exponentially multiplies it for his purposes.

Don had a dream. What do you have? Is it a skill? Is it mastery of a certain field or industry? Is it money? Property? Connections? An art? Or is it a dream that's something like Don's? Put another way, what is that in your hand?

The vision I want you to gain is a way of seeing what you have as valuable. Remember that Don was almost embarrassed by his dream. How unlikely it was! How beyond him! Yet millions have been helped and millions more will be because Don Stephens courageously acted on his dream.

This is how it works, my friend. This is what it means to recognize the value of what you have and invest it for the good of others. Thank God for Mother Teresa. Thank God for Don Stephens. Thank God for Mercy Ships. And thank God even more that he is a promise-keeping God who will expand what we invest in his kingdom to accomplish great things.

Chapter 6

Everyone Can Do Something

It is vanity to love that which passeth away, and not to hasten where eternal joy abideth.

—Thomas á Kempis

There is a truth in the Bible that is one of the hardest for us human beings to get settled in our souls. It is the idea that God uses everything in our lives—the good and the bad, the painful and the glorious, the agonizing and the triumphant—to fulfill his purposes.

It is a difficult truth for us because we live much of our lives trying to avoid pain. We hope to escape tragedy, to sidestep disaster. Yet they come nevertheless, and then we are told that God can use them. How can it be? How can the things that make us weep and force us to suffer through dark nights of the soul be tools in the hands of a loving God to complete our destined purpose? It simply is not something we humans will ever fully understand in this life. Yet it is true. Here is that very truth from the pages of Scripture: "And we know that for those who love God all things work together for good, for those who are called according to his purpose" (Rom. 8:28).

I mention this because it is at the heart of the story I want to tell you next. It is ultimately a tale of millions of lives changed, but it starts in tragedy, in a horrifying saga of death and poverty and struggle. It is tender to me because the man who lived it is a dear friend, one of the most unassuming yet faithful men I know. His name is Hal Donaldson.

My friend grew up the son of a pastor and his wife. Love enveloped Hal and his three siblings completely in their early years. They were taught to give themselves to God with passion and to serve people with devotion. Hal's parents modeled these virtues in all they did.

In fact, it was out of just such devotion that the family of six piled into their car on August 25, 1969. Hal was twelve at the time. There was a church business meeting to attend, and it wouldn't do for the pastor to be late. The four children were squirming and resistant, dreading the boredom that surely lay ahead. Rescue came, though, when Mom and Dad caught sight of the babysitter in the rearview mirror. The car stopped and the children piled out, grateful for the deliverance that had befallen them. Mom and Dad drove on to their meeting.

It was later that night that a knock came on the door of the family home. There had been an accident, two uniformed policemen gently explained. A drunk driver had hit the family car head on. The children's father was dead. Their mother was in a hospital fighting for her life.

It was the kind of news on which destinies turn. Neighbors gathered at the house, concerned and grieving. The police asked, "Can anyone take the children tonight? Otherwise, we'll have to take them down to the station."

There was silence as the meaning of what had happened registered in every heart. Who could take four children in such circumstances? What would happen if no one stepped up? Surely, it was all too much to ask of those who had their own to care for.

The silence was piercing, and then a voice came from within the crowd: "We'll take them." It was Bill Davis. He and his wife, Louvada, lived in a single-wide trailer with their four children. Yet here they were, stepping into the lives of the Donaldson children, offering what they had for those in need.

It was a moment of grace, but it came at a price. The ten of them—the Davises and the Donaldsons—lived together in that trailer for nearly a year. There weren't enough beds; the children took turns sleeping on the floor. And the food barely stretched to meet the need. Yet they survived, and the healing kindness of the Davis family marked Hal for the rest of his life.

In time, Hal's mother was released from the hospital. She started working to support her family. Though she gave it her best, it was seldom enough. The family had to rely on food stamps and the generosity of neighbors. Hal had to carry responsibility far beyond his years. In high school, he pumped gas and changed tires to help the family survive.

The experience of poverty tormented him. He yearned to escape it. After graduation, he landed a job at Dow Chemical while he pursued a degree in journalism. He hoped that his talent as a writer would help him rise above what he had known. And it did. He wrote. He gained some renown. He prospered. He outstripped the grind of his youth.

Then came the writing assignment that changed his life. He was sent to Calcutta, India, to do research for a book on the missionary/statesman Mark Buntain. Someone suggested that there was a woman in town who could provide a unique perspective. Hal must meet her, he was told. Her name was Mother Teresa.

Hal was overwhelmed. He knew of the legendary nun, of course, but he had never thought he would meet her. Then the moment came. He arrived at the Home for the Dying Destitutes and waited for Mother Teresa to arrive.

When she appeared, she was wearing her distinctive white-and-blue sari. She shuffled when she approached, as was appropriate for her age.

"What's your name, young man?" she asked.

"Hal Donaldson," her visitor managed.

"Where are you from, and what do you do?" she asked with her trademark directness.

"I'm a writer from the United States. I came to Calcutta to write a book on Mark and Huldah Buntain."

The nun's face lit up. "They have helped many in our city!" she exclaimed.

"Yes, they have big hearts," Hal agreed. "May I ask you a few questions?"

"If it will help them in their work," Mother Teresa replied evenly.

The interview unfolded over the next twenty minutes. Hal later remembered thinking, *I feel like I'm talking to my grandmother—without the milk and cookies—rather than a recipient of the Nobel Peace Prize.*

He also remembered that each time he praised Mother Teresa, she said, "It's all because of God."

As the interview drew to a close, Mother Teresa, as she had so many times before, decided to push into the soul before her.

"Young man, can I ask you what you do to help the poor?"

She wasn't pressing a case. She wasn't accusing. She was trying to unearth something she surely sensed lurking in Hal's heart. He remembers thinking that if he lied to Mother Teresa, he would likely put himself in danger of going to hell!

"I'm really not doing anything," he said with more sadness than perhaps he intended.

There was a pause. The painful kind. Then Mother Teresa smiled and said with piercing kindness, "Everyone can do something."

The words seemed more than the end of a conversation. They were an epitaph over all that Hal had seen in India and much that he had known back in the states. The sight of children living in hovels. Of nasty drinking water filled with sewage. Of children climbing on garbage heaps. Of the flies and the disease and the deformities and the corpses.

Hal returned to his luxury hotel. He rested in his plush bed and let his eyes fall on the crystal and the brass that adorned his opulent room. He dined on the finest food. Yet each night, he heard Calcutta's sick and dying moan their misery as though to him alone.

A question began to form in Hal's mind. It was born of the streets of Calcutta and that knock on the door those years before, of Mother Teresa's question and the humiliation of his family's torturous years. It was this: "What is holding me back from becoming the revolutionary I was born to be?"

Hal flew home to California. He had already made the decisions of a lifetime. He had already become a changed man. Soon after he returned, he filled a pickup truck with groceries and began giving them out to families in need. It wasn't all that he wanted to do, but it was something, and he sensed it was a beginning.

Looking back years later, the man in that pickup with Mother Teresa's words ringing in his ears was just then taking the first steps toward founding Convoy of Hope, one of the most successful firms addressing poverty in the world today.

"Everyone can do something," Mother Teresa had said. So Hal did. It began as little more than a vision and a prayer. He created local events to provide food for the poor. He used his writing and speaking skills to rally people to his vision. He borrowed trucks and even warehouse space from other organizations. People were fed. Lives were changed. Hope spread.

But it was all on a relatively small level at first. Then churches, businesses, civic groups, and even government departments began to get involved. In time, Convoy could buy its own tractor-trailers capable of crisscrossing the country to deliver food and emergency supplies to those in need. If there was a hurricane or some other type of disaster, Convoy was there. If a community was hard-hit, Hal's team appeared.

Let me jump to today to tell you the astonishing statistics that capture the impact of the story. Then I'm going to tell you some of the things I most admire about Convoy. Just let these numbers sink in. Since 1994, Convoy has helped more than 115 million people. They have served more than 327 million meals. More than 622,000 volunteers have been mobilized in the United States alone. They have worked in 126 countries and distributed food and supplies worth more than $971 million.

Since my goal in telling you these numbers is to celebrate what God has done and to inspire you, let me ask you to use your imagination for a moment. Imagine Hal flying back from India. Visualize him playing Mother Teresa's words over and over again in his mind. Then picture his eagerness to land in California, find a pickup truck, and take a load of food to a needy family. One man. One sentence. One truck. One single purpose.

Now remind yourself of the scope of the organization today. Think of the 126 countries, 622,000 volunteers in the United States, and 115 million people served. How has it all been possible? You know my answer already. It is because Hal Donaldson courageously used his talents to make a difference in the world. Now he will be the first to tell you that Convoy is far beyond him.

This is how it works, my friend. This is what God does. This is the meaning of the Parable of the Talents.

Yet let me tell you some of the things I most admire about folks at Convoy. They are smart. They are strategic. They involve brilliant people in getting beyond delivering food to making substantive differences in entire regions of the world.

For example, they have a fantastic women's empowerment

program. They realize that in much of the world, it is the women who shape the culture of the home and thus the culture of entire villages and regions. It is also the women who are the greatest untapped resource. So they provide job training and education. They train women in entrepreneurial skills. Many of the women they've worked with now own their own businesses and can feed and care for their own children for the first time. Their futures grow brighter every day.

One of the things my firm, Westfall Gold, does when working with an organization is to create powerful videos of the people being served and the progress being made. You should see the videos of the women Convoy serves. Their faces are beaming. They are grateful and tenderly proud. Often, they tell our interviewers that they are the first in their family lines to own their own businesses or to be self-supporting or to have a hope of sending their children to good schools or perhaps of even owning their own homes. It is all because of the gifts God has given these women and the wisdom of Convoy of Hope in drawing those gifts out and helping them become marketable. All this is done, of course, with a deeply and vibrantly Christian approach.

There is another ingenious initiative of Convoy, and it is one I admit that I sometimes do not understand but that I admire deeply. It is their agricultural effort. This involves some cutting-edge science that I often can't follow, but it is changing lives the world over.

In general, this agricultural effort is about equipping struggling farmers with training, tools, and seeds so they can produce life-sustaining crops. These in turn translate into thousands of meals and vital income.

Yet they also bring the science I've mentioned into play. The man I enjoy watching in this effort is Dr. Jason Streubel. They call him "Dr. Dirt." This man is so passionate about his field—dirt!—that I've seen him repeatedly light up a room during our Donor Weekends. Sophisticated people actually spend entire meals talking about what they've learned about dirt. It is amazing!

Dr. Streubel makes the simple but profound point that "agriculture starts with the dirt." Decked out in his Wrangler jeans, steel-toed, three-quarter-shank work boots, and the Indiana Jones hat he bought at Disneyland, Dr. Streubel is usually preaching this message while walking farm fields around the world.

He is making a difference. He and his Convoy agricultural team are usually faced with generations of bad agricultural practices that are robbing the land, limiting crop yields, and even endangering human health. Instead, they offer wise, modern solutions and tools. After education programs are conducted in local churches and community centers, farmers are given virus-resistant seeds. They are given new tools. Convoy advisors help local farmers implement what they've learned in their training: how to farm without pesticides, how to keep costs low, how to protect the environment and human health. Soil quality improves; crops are better able to resist the challenges of weather, pests, and viruses; and fields become lush.

Then there are the unusual practices that produce tremendous results. Dr. Streubel urges farmers—in Haiti, for example—to handpick caterpillars off their plants. It is an admittedly tedious, tiring, and sometimes gooey process. Yet fields can be decimated by these creatures, and Dr. Streubel explains to farmers why this is so and how the solution is within their skill set.

It all sounds so simple. Yet you should see the fields in Haiti where the Convoy agricultural team has been training and providing tools. To quote a Convoy report, "In all directions, fields are brimming with corn, maize, okra, sorghum, black beans, and pigeon peas." A local pastor confirms that "before the project started this valley was empty, but now all you see is crops in every direction. Our people are very happy and proud of this."

What does Convoy require in return? They ask each farmer to give 10 percent of their harvest to the Convoy of Hope Children's Feeding Initiative in their region. Often, this means that these farmers are feeding their own children as well as the children of their communities.

I would be proud of Convoy and Dr. Streubel if they were simply delivering food and supplies where they were needed around the world. They've gone beyond this, though. They are smart. They change the systems that produce poverty and want. In every way, they make barren fields lush.

As with some of the other organizations I've described, I get to see the courage and character of Convoy from behind the scenes. I tend to get introduced once the firm is successful but is dreaming of a greater impact than their current income affords. So I get to see an organization's leaders "on the stretch," feeling the call to greater things but also the constraints of their resources.

This was how I came upon Convoy, and I remember it well. My initial connection was a man who has now become a dear friend: Dan Clark, Convoy's vice-president for partner development. I remember that Dan invited me to make a presentation to some of their leadership about the Westfall Gold model. Convoy leaders were nothing but polite, but I could tell that our approach pushed them a bit. Normally, I talk about three-day events and five-star hotels and giving gifts to major donors. Convoy didn't have much of a major donor program at the time, so all this was new and a bit challenging.

What followed was a real revelation of who they are, and Dan Clark tells it better than I do. Later, he said of my presentation,

> [It] pushed us outside our comfort zone, especially in terms of the five-star resorts. It was pushing us to do

things we had never done before. At first glance, we just didn't have the stomach for it.

We tried to do a hybrid event, a golf event we already had a contract for. So we opted to do two nights, not three, at a four-star resort, not five. Bob was gracious enough to say, "Yes, we'll give it a try. We'll work with you and wish you the best, even though we have concerns." So we went into it and spent $150,000. We raised about $450,000. So we didn't lose money. We got a return.

Yet to the credit of the Convoy team, they realized that such returns could not carry them to the greater global impact they knew they were called to. They did some soul-searching. Here's Dan again: "It forced this gut-check moment with our management team and board. And we said, 'OK, if we're gonna do this, we're going all in. Let's do it the Westfall way.' And so we did. That next year, we followed the recipe and had our first Westfall event. We spent a half-million dollars and raised nearly three. After that, there was no looking back."

Let me report what happened over the next few years, and then I'll tell you the underlying reason for it all. The year after Convoy did that first full Westfall event, they got an eight-to-one return on their investment and raised $5.4 million. The third year, it was nine-to-one on their investment with $8.2 million raised. The fourth, it was eleven-to-one with $13.2 million raised. And so it went. I leave the exact tracking of numbers to my team, but I can tell you that we now regularly do events with Convoy that raise more than $25 million a year.

Now, remember that I work with money, and so I report kingdom principles in financial terms. But let your imagination run again. Picture the children's feeding centers that are being built around the world. Picture desiccated fields becoming lush with nourishing food. Picture disaster scenes after floods and hurricanes, droughts and pestilence, and then the restoration that begins once Convoy ships and trucks arrive. Picture those 115 million people who have been served doubling or tripling in number. See, this is what that money raised means, and these scenes are never far from my mind. They move, inspire, and power me onward.

I'm proud of Convoy for all they've accomplished, but I'm perhaps most stirred by the courage factor I've seen among their leadership. Listen to how Dan Clark reported it recently:

> Courage is a necessary trait for any fundraiser. It's necessary to have a healthy dose of courage pumping through your veins to do this work because the law of harvest is that "you reap what you sow." Sow sparingly and you reap sparingly.

But if you sow generously, you will reap the same. And it takes guts—courage, if you will—to sow generously. There's just no other way about it. So yes, it took courage on the part of our leaders and everyone who was involved. It took courage for me to ask and courage for the board to say yes.

Here's what I know from years of experience. Courage like the kind found at the heart of Convoy will reproduce itself in the lives of those they serve. It will spread. It will multiply. And lives will be changed by that courage to live out the Parable of the Talents on a global scale.

Now, you already know what is coming your way! I've got to ask you, what is your version of the Hal Donaldson story? Where are you meant to live out the courage that we've seen at the heart of Convoy? Please, find it. Please, cry out to God to guide you to the field in which you are meant to invest. You may not be called to build a Convoy, but you can make your life a channel of hope in the arena you are meant to impact. Remember the words of Mother Teresa: "Everyone can do something."

I also want to bring us back to where we began. The Hal Donaldson story began in tragedy. There was pain and loneliness and lack. Out of these ashes, God built something astonishing through a man who was willing. It may be that you are sitting in ashes as you read these words. You may doubt that anything of value can ever be made of your life or your investment in others. The stories in this book say otherwise. The truth of God's Word definitely says otherwise. It's there on nearly every page. You invest what you've been given. You put yourself in a position of increase. God will reward. God will grant joy. God will reposition you. That's not Bob Westfall talking. That is our promise-keeping God!

Chapter 7

The Poet-Warriors

To find out what one is fitted to do, and to secure an opportunity to do it, is the key to happiness.

—John Dewey

I t's the magnificence of the people that gets to me. It's what a man or a woman goes through to step out of the norm and to do something courageous for God. I never cease to be moved by it. Because I've been there, I can almost feel each story I hear.

It starts with the birth of a possibility somewhere deep in the heart. There is the pondering, the prayer, the deliberating over what it all might mean. Faith starts to rise. Then there is sharing it with those nearby. Some jump right in. Some oppose. Always, there is the struggle.

There are also hidden forces in the soul that no one else knows—the insecurities, the hauntings of past failures, the self-doubts. Courage comes, though, and the investment is made. It doesn't stop there. Evil opposes. Simple human nature gets in the way. Still, the valiant soul soldiers on. There are the sleepless nights and the fears that taunt and the hopes that are cradled deep inside where no one can see.

And victory comes. The day of breakthrough. The day of celebration. Lives are changed. God has kept his promise.

I don't cry easily, but these stories get me. I can hardly speak of them without tearing up. It happens so much that I'm often teased about it. I don't mind. I hope I'm always captivated by the idea of a life invested in a glorious cause.

I get to see many great victories because of the work I do. I also get to see the struggles these victories require, the heroic personal battles. It has changed me and made me treat people differently. It has also given me a special place in my heart for those who fight great battles to do noble things. Let me tell you about a few of these, about the beauty of these poet-warriors.

Alan Gold: Stranger in a Strange Land

One of the most unusual men I know is Alan Gold. I say that with love, and I can get away with it because Alan is the reason for the word "Gold" in the name of our firm, Westfall Gold. I don't mean that symbolically. That's his name on the sign! Alan is a president and the creative chief in our firm. He's an amazing gift. He also has a fascinating story.

It is consistent with the many oddities of Alan's life that he knows when he was conceived. It was on board a freighter from Darwin, Australia, to Singapore in 1956. The audacious young Alan asked his mother about it once. She did the math and told him. This tells us much about them both, doesn't it?

Alan's parents were nearly the ideal picture of intrepid missionaries. As a young man, his father had lived as the lone Westerner in a village in the Golden Triangle of Thailand. The village was a two-day walk from the nearest road. He would routinely park his Land Rover by the road and hike the many rugged miles just to get to his hut.

Alan's parents met and married in New York while his dad was on furlough there. Then he took his new wife back to Australia. This required taking a ship across the ocean, a train across the stark Australian Outback, and another boat to get them to their destination. It was all preamble to a rugged, sacrificing life together.

By the time Alan was born, the family served God in Thailand. Though his family life was tender and loving, Alan remembers the struggles they had because of the treatment they received from home. There were the political tensions in missions organizations and the near disregard for the sacrifices of a missionary family. People would send used tea bags, already opened food, and unclean clothes to the missionary servants on the front lines for the gospel of Jesus. Such things seep into the heart of a little boy, forming in Alan's case a questioning, skeptical cast on the world.

Because it was the policy of his parents' religious denomination, Alan was forced to leave his family and was sent away to boarding school when he came of age. However well-intentioned this policy may have been, it made for a traumatic, even alienating experience for Alan. He describes it all these years later as like being in foster care. It was an often-soulless institutional life wrapped in an often-harsh religiosity. He was once punished merely for playing cards. The sting of it remains until this day.

There is an old joke that you know you are a missionary kid if you're reading *National Geographic* magazine and you see people you know. Alan's life was nearly this way. He lived on a constantly changing landscape fashioned by new schools, global travels, and international parents. It was often disorienting, but it left the gifted Alan with an adventurous spirit. He was also impressed with the lives of those around him. Nearly everyone he knew was giving their all to change the world. Everyone was invested, sacrificing.

This kept the question of where Alan would invest his own life ever before him. His intellectual prowess landed him in fine schools. He studied at Westmont College and eventually found himself in a PhD program at Emory University in Atlanta. Yet his varied religious experience caused him to know that he didn't want to be a missionary and that he probably did not want to work in churches. What would he do? What gifts did he have to invest?

These questions plagued him while he was also plagued by being a stranger in his own home country. This came with some hilarious results. He was only a few years from Thailand when he began college, and so he was quite naïve about American ways. A friend invited him to a toga-themed party. In the days leading up to the party, there was a great deal of joking about vestal virgins and such. Alan didn't quite understand this brand of American sarcasm and so took the whole matter seriously. He didn't want to be involved with anything involving vestal virgins, and so he began asking about what was going to happen at the party and how it would all be done. Fortunately for Alan, his friends took his questions as more joking and ignored him. He was a stranger in a strange land, and it took years for him to feel remotely at home. Alan jokes that he still hasn't settled in, even all these years later!

He planned to carve out a career in academia but quickly became disillusioned with that often stiff and arid culture. At just about that time, his mother began working for World Relief and learned of a job in the ad agency that produced World Relief's commercials. Alan applied. Trying to make the right impression in his interview, he wore a black suit. Trust me, that is probably the last time Alan Gold has ever appeared anywhere in a suit! The irony is, though, that the people interviewing him assumed that Alan couldn't be the creative person they were looking for—precisely because he wore black suits!

Still, they gave Alan a copy test, he was typically brilliant, and he got the job. Though he may not have known it, he was just stepping onto the stage of his destiny. He worked at that ad firm for a year and then took a job with CNN. He had wild experiences laboring in the vicinity of the ever-nonconforming Ted Turner, founder of CNN, and then he moved on to other leading ad agencies.

It is often said that the children of missionaries and perhaps military brats—those who are ever on the move in their early lives—are abroad for the rest of their days. They seldom feel planted. They put out vines but don't put down roots. Alan felt this. And while he wrestled with life and belonging and being in place, he was growing. He was learning. He was acquiring the skills that, along with his intelligence, made him an exceptional man.

Yet his work in secular ad agencies left him unfulfilled. He was successful but not fully using his gifts, competent but not complete. He was a self-described quirky person with a rebellious streak who had a foot in the religious world and a foot in secular society, a man who was ever asking himself, "Where does this mess fit?"

It was just at this time when Alan was achieving but searching that I began considering him for my firm. I had first met Alan in 1992 when he helped me on a contract basis in my work for Walk Thru the Bible. By 2006, I needed someone of Alan's gifts. I knew he was talented but also had an outlier personality. It didn't bother me. I'm at home with strange, to tell the truth. So I asked Alan to join me.

Here is what moves me, and this is why I tell you this story. In the tales we often hear of great success, of people investing their gifts, we usually move quickly from first steps to great accomplishment in two sentences. We skip over the hardship. We skip over insecurities and embarrassment and the years of contending with what we are and what we are not but wish we were.

Today, Alan Gold handles the creative side of our firm, having worked with more than 120 clients, traveling the world, and recording their stories in some of the most powerful videos you will ever see. We have reached a billion dollars raised and will go on to greater milestones as much because of Alan's gifts as any other factor. We couldn't do it without him.

Yet imagine the insecurities of a missionary child dumped in fast-paced American society. Imagine the lonely boy in emotionally barren boarding schools. Imagine being pressed between your religious roots and your secular success. Imagine being ever abroad.

What I love about Alan's story is the way God uses his unique experiences to touch so many lives today. You see, all of Alan's travels, all of his study, all of his varied religious influences have made him capable of getting to the heart of what our clients need, of what the transforming nature of a given story really is.

I remember something a client of ours said about their experience with Alan years ago. When they first met him, they said it was like meeting a "mad scientist." They were probably referring to Alan's head of white hair, his full white beard, and his manner. Yet they also said that things they had wrestled with as a firm for years, things that were tangled and confused, were straightened out in an hour. Why? Because Alan Gold's unique past gave him the ability to see what others do not see. I love the way God makes the hardships of our past redemptive and of use in the present. This is also what I admire about Alan Gold's life.

Now, trust me, Alan is still a nonconformist to this day. I still can't get him to wear a suit for a big meeting, and he is still likely to press me about climate change on a ride to the airport. What's more, Alan will tell you himself that he is still an outlier, still a bit rebellious.

Yet he has put his gifts in play. He has invested himself. He does as his parents modeled for him and serves a greater good with all he's been given. And lives have been changed as a result—hundreds of millions of them.

Alan Gold is living out the Parable of the Talents and doing it magnificently. He is also, let me tell you, one of the coolest cats I know!

Burt Rosen: Father to the Lost

Thinking back to when I asked Alan Gold to join my firm reminds me of one of our first clients. It was Knox Area Rescue Ministries (a.k.a. KARM, referred to earlier in this book), led by Burt Rosen. This man's story is one of the most agonizing I know and yet one filled with impact. It will change you.

Every year, on October 15, there is a huge celebration in the outside courtyard of KARM in Knoxville, Tennessee. It is a birthday party intended to heal souls. In other words, it is a party for loved ones who are missing or for those who weren't around for birthday parties but should have been or for those who simply need someone to say "Happy Birthday" to them. There is someone missing from this party, though. He has been for years. It is the son of Burt Rosen, KARM's executive director. But before I tell you that tale, let me tell you about Burt.

This man is high energy in shoes. He never stops, hardly ever slows down. It is because his cause is huge, and he knows he can make a difference. So he invests himself—fully. It wasn't always this way.

Burt was born in Miami, Florida, and describes himself as an Eddie Haskell figure in his early years, using the name of the irritating kid in the 1950s TV show *Leave It to Beaver*. Eddie was not a likable character, but he knew how to schmooze the parents of his friends. Burt was the same, he says. He was shaped by the fact that his parents' broken marriage left him poor, and he constantly felt the insecurities of a boy who had two pairs of pants and two shirts to his name.

To provide for himself, he sold drugs. Then he began taking drugs. His life was a painful descent until, on January 1, 1973, Burt, who had been raised Jewish, decided to follow Jesus Christ. Soon after, he naïvely shared what had happened to him with his Jewish boss. He was promptly fired. The man thought he had gone insane. Burt started volunteering at a small halfway house in the inner city of Miami. There he began learning about the challenges faced by men coming out of prison. In time, he joined Charles Colson's Prison Fellowship. He loved this work and gave himself to it. It took him from Miami to Louisville, Kentucky, and then to Washington, DC.

There were painful episodes along the way. Burt's wife, Carolyn, was diagnosed with cancer. Surgery saved her, but sometime later, she was also in a horrible automobile accident. She could easily have died, and recovery was long. Though Carolyn is a warrior at Burt's side today, these experiences changed Burt. They made his heart tender and even more sensitive to those suffering and alone.

While working for Prison Fellowship, Burt learned of a position at KARM. He resisted it. He told the man who gave him the information about the job, "That's just not on the radar screen for us." The man asked if he would pray about the matter. It is typical of my friend Burt that he replied, "Oh, crap! I wish you hadn't asked me that!"

What followed is more hilarious if Burt tells it than if I do. The brief version is that he took the job. Once he stepped into the role, he got an unwanted education. KARM would close its fiscal year sixty days later almost $700,000 in the red. It had a $500,000 line of credit that was exhausted, a donor program and a major gift program that had flatlined, and two thrift stores that were losing $100,000 a year. Burt was surprised but undaunted. He knew what he was called to do.

Let me skip ahead. Burt has led KARM powerfully through the years. Today, their facilities are stellar. They serve one thousand meals a day. In fact, they are the only organization in Knoxville that serves a free breakfast, lunch, and dinner every day of the year. Nearly four hundred people stay at the KARM facility every night. Beyond all this, KARM offers job training, employment assistance, help for displaced families, aid to victims of domestic violence, literacy programs, counseling services, rehabilitation programs, and many other services too numerous to list. Always there are the worship opportunities and Bible instruction and prayer meetings that keep KARM alive and vital with love and God's spirit. I can't tell you how proud I am of them and how privileged I feel to have them as a client.

But I haven't told you the heart of the story yet.

You see, Burt and Carolyn have a son named Matthew.

He's the oldest of the four Rosen children, and he was the one that they could count on to always excel—in academics, in sports, in life as a whole. His dream was to play football for the University of Miami Hurricanes, and that's what he did. His parents expected a stellar college career and even greater heights thereafter.

Then the trouble started. Matthew suddenly left school. He enrolled in Virginia Tech. His second year there, he dropped out. He returned home to live with his parents, and life with him became a living hell, Burt recalls. Matthew was angry, abusive, and obsessed. The other family members looked for excuses to stay away from home. Carolyn began to fear for her life. It was all torment all the time. The Rosens took counsel with a friend they had known in Prison Fellowship. He said the terrible words Burt and Carolyn already knew were true: "You have given up control of your home to your son, and if you don't ask him to go, you are jeopardizing the rest of the family."

Soon after, they asked their son to leave their home. Burt recalls that moment vividly: "We watched Matthew walk down the street with his roller-board suitcase as we sobbed our eyes out, wondering what had happened to our son."

The story did not end there. Matthew enrolled in other colleges. There was always trouble. He was arrested. Burt and Carolyn would get him out of jail and take him home. The trouble would always return. Matthew disappeared finally, and in time, the Rosens heard that he was living on the streets of New York. God did miracles to help them find him, and then soon after, he disappeared again.

Matthew is now completely gone from his parents' lives. They haven't seen him in decades. They assume he is on the streets somewhere if he is even alive. They do not know, cannot be sure, but still, they pray and hope.

While Burt and Carolyn hope against hope for the return of their troubled prodigal son, they love others in his name. As Burt recently told our team, "I don't know if I'll ever get to see Matthew again, but every day, there's close to four hundred or more just like him who walk through our doors. I'm obsessed with this idea, and I'm determined to spend myself in changing their lives."

There it is. Against the pain, against the uncertainty, against the challenges, Burt Rosen invests his gifts in the lives of other people's sons while his own is lost to him. He is, then, a father to the lost, both to the four hundred who enter KARM every day and to the one he and his wife always hope will return. Do you see why I can hardly think of a man like Burt without tears in my eyes, why I am determined to help him touch as many lives as God will give him? This man lives out my favorite parable and does it despite the pain. What a hero he is.

Scott Olson: Rewinding the Script

I'll tell this tale briefly, but I cannot think of Burt Rosen's story without thinking of Scott Olson. Both men took over failing organizations, invested their lives, and so brought change to millions of people.

Scott is a Renaissance man. He is a university professor. He has run a business. He's also a musician who loves playing jazz. Before he even came to the organization I'm going to tell you about, he already had twenty-five years of international leadership experience. I love Scott for all these reasons, but also because he is a hard-hitting, sometimes tough-talking leader. I relate to him. I admire his intensity.

In May of 2008, he took over the leadership of an organization called iTeams. By his own admission, the ship he boarded at that time was sinking. Just the year before, the board of the organization had met in Costa Rica and had decided by only one vote to keep iTeams alive. They were financially broken and internally rudderless. Adding to it all, Scott came and took the lead just as the devastation of the 2008 U.S. financial crisis was dawning. As Scott recalls, "We had zero major donors. Everybody had left us. It was definitely hard times."

While other missions organizations were dying, Scott was determined that iTeams would rise. Yet what did he have to invest that God could use? He had experience. He had vision. He had grit. He also had a deep knowledge of Scripture. He put all this into play.

He and his team decided they had to return to the "Ancient Path." By this, they meant the example of Jesus, the methods found in Scripture. Scott was weary of seeing Christian organizations conform to every new idea thrown out at every trendy leadership conference. He wanted iTeams to build on solid truths that worked.

His innovations were more numerous than I can track here. The core change he made, though, was to join missionary work with the compassionate and practical meeting of people's needs. He had seen these two efforts increasingly divorced from each other in modern Christianity. He intended to wed them again and to do so from within communities around the world. His firm would become a vision-driven, innovative effort to capture hearts by meeting needs and to do so as part of their communities rather than as visitors from the outside. In short, in his words, he "rewound the script," took Jesus as his model, and refashioned the entire organization accordingly.

Sure, people left. Sure, there was tension and heartache. There was also the long slog back to financial health, which Westfall Gold was privileged to help with. Yet they did it. The ministry is now known as One Collective and is thriving by touching lives, healing souls, and meeting needs the world over. In forty communities around the world, One Collective is bringing people together to help the oppressed.

I want you to celebrate this with Scott, but I also want you to hear from his lips something of the price: "This twelve-year journey has cost me almost everything. It was that hard. It has been the hardest thing of my life leading this organization through this."

I don't share this with you to discourage you. Remember that I'm here to impart courage! Yet I don't want to hide from you that sometimes we are called to do hard things to see great things done. Sometimes investing our gifts calls for a struggle. I don't want you to be surprised. And I want you to be inspired by the poet-warriors who have gone before you and shown us all how to battle on tirelessly until victory is won.

Katie Davis Majors and Doug Martin: An Amazima Story

If you've already read Katie Davis's *New York Times* best-selling book *Kisses from Katie*, then you know this outrageous story. If you haven't read this book, get it. You will marvel. You will reflect. Then, I trust, you'll get busy!

I won't tell the whole story here so as not to ruin it for you. Yet I can't offer even a brief list of people I admire for using their talents without reflecting for a moment on Katie Davis.

She was just a teenager from Nashville. She wanted to do

missionary work and thought that working at an orphanage was the best fit. She had no particular place in mind, but an orphanage in Uganda replied to her inquiries. As teenagers tend to do, she bugged her parents incessantly until finally her mother agreed to visit the orphanage with her during the Christmas break of Katie's senior year of high school. If all seemed in place, she intended to take a gap year before going to college and serve at this same orphanage.

Katie soon found herself in the land of her destiny. It was the children who won her over. Orphans in Uganda are often children with parents who simply can't afford to keep them. Ultimately Katie decided to leave her life in the United States and care for the children she met. Being the intrepid lady she is, she didn't just work at an orphanage. She became a mother to fifteen children, thirteen girls and two boys. She also married a man named Benji Majors, who is as given to the cause as Katie is.

That's not all. They have purchased seventy acres of land just outside of Jinja, Uganda. Already, there are forty-five buildings on the property, including fifteen for student housing, eleven for latrines, a chapel, and three classroom blocks. They have 220 students on campus now and take in 72 new students each year. They also operate feeding programs, farming outreach programs, and a medical outreach program. Trust me, my firm intends to do all it can to make sure this is just the beginning.

Their organization is called Amazima Ministries

International. *Amazima* means "truth" in Luganda, one of the languages spoken in Uganda. And here is the truth I want you to see in Katie's story. She had to break from the norm. She had to leave her comfortable life in Nashville. She surrendered her preferences and gave herself to orphans in a country not her own. She also put her gifts into play and grew something stunning, something that is changing lives in Uganda. With her books and through her example, she is changing lives around the world too. My point is that a teenage girl used her talents to make a difference in the lives of others. And look at what God has done.

Also amazing? As I write these words, Katie has just now turned thirty-one. God alone knows what he intends for the next decades in Katie's life. But I am sure these decades will be filled with even more examples of this young lady putting her talents to work. May we all do the same.

By the way, there is an inspiring tale within the Amazima journey. Doug Martin, Amazima's managing director in the United States, has lived out the Parable of the Talents in an astonishing way. You see, he left a highly prosperous career to serve in ministry, to maximize his gifts for God, and this led to his current role with Amazima.

His story moves me. Doug worked for a government think tank early in his career and then became a leader in the tech boom of the 1990s. He prospered as he helped grow his lucrative firm. While he did this, he and his wife began volunteering for a national marriage and family ministry. Using his gifts to serve people began to change him. Increasingly, he wondered why he was traveling the world for business when his heart was more and more consumed with ministry.

Finally, in a dramatic move, he and his wife decided to "walk away from the business world," as Doug says. They moved to Little Rock, Arkansas, and then to Nashville, Tennessee, serving in ministries as they did. Doug was so eager to touch lives for God that he even attended a seminary in Nashville. He was following his heart, the dream he had long carried to put his gifts and talents into play for the kingdom of God.

It was as they studied and served and ministered in Nashville that Doug and his wife met Katie Davis. They got to know Amazima and follow its thrilling rise. They also connected to Amazima's vision for children, since Doug and his wife had adopted children themselves and knew the transforming power of it.

In time, Doug took a role with Amazima, and he has brought all his fire and passion with him into that great cause. I want you to hear him describe this in his own terms:

I've always said that at the end of the game, I want to be the guy who goes out with the dirty uniform. Spent. On a stretcher with the IVs in me. I don't want to finish this game clean and neat. I want to be all in, full-on, leaving it all on the field. I believe that's the life of faith God has called each of us to. And you know what? That means we may make some mistakes. We may trip and fall over some things. But we'll never be accused of taking the easy way out and leaving work undone.

This is the passion of my friend Doug Martin, and this is what moved him to leave a lucrative life in business to use his gifts for God. He is now part of the exciting Amazima story as it changes lives throughout the world. Yet it has all come about as common people courageously gave themselves to heroic purposes and saw their investment increase for the good of others. It is an honor to even know them.

Think back on the stories I've told in this chapter. There is Alan Gold, a brilliant man who has had to push past his own alienation to use his gifts to the full. Now hundreds of millions of souls are helped by the work he does. No one is more grateful than I am, since Alan serves at Westfall Gold.

There is also Burt Rosen, the father to thousands whose own son is lost to him. Yet he has used his gifts to change lives. He told me recently that he is inspired by the words of the eminent pastor Joseph Garlington. Pastor Garlington said, "The opportunity of a lifetime must be seized in the lifetime of the opportunity." Burt is seizing his opportunities to do good in the world while those opportunities are present. How I love and admire him.

Then there is Scott Olson, an already accomplished man who took over a sinking organization in a sinking economy. Yet his vision, his devotion to Scripture, and his toughness as a leader carried the day and produced forty transforming communities around the world. He "rewound the script," rediscovered the "Ancient Path," and is still making history.

Finally, there is young Katie Davis Majors. Today, she has a huge property in Uganda, a famous family of adopted children, and two *New York Times* best-selling books. Yet originally, there was only a teenage girl with a heart to serve. A girl who had gifts to give. And she was willing to put it all into play for the glory of God.

My point is this: There is no perfect person making the perfect investment at the perfect time and place producing a perfect result. There is only a perfect God. We take what we have been given, what we are made for, and we invest and use it for good. We maximize as we can. It is God who gives the increase. It is God who puts us in a heightened position. It is God who changes the world with what we have given him.

So I've written this chapter for your encouragement. You have gifts. You have the interest and the will if you have stuck with me this far into these pages. God is working. You are pondering a course of action in your heart. Don't let the possible challenges or your possible imperfections—or those of the situation you are in—keep you from taking the bold steps you are called to. Trust that God has given you what he has "according to your ability," as the Parable of the Talents tells us. And trust that he is with you as you act.

Chapter 8

A Valiant Work in Progress

The artist is nothing without the gift, but the gift is nothing without work.

—Emile Zola

So far in this book, I've told you stories about people and organizations that have achieved a remarkable level of success. There will be more achievement coming—and I'm invested in nearly all of them to help make sure this is true—but each story has already reached a mountaintop, perhaps the first of many.

Before I offer you some final insights and perhaps wisdom for your own journey in the last chapter of this book, I want to tell you about a woman who has only recently launched into her cause. Though she already had a remarkable career prior to taking on this challenge, she has chosen to invest herself—for the rest of her life, she tells me—in rescuing lives from one of the most troubling evils of our age.

The evil I'm talking about is human trafficking. The organization designed to address it is called Uncaged. And the amazing woman who has set herself to combat it is Kim Westfall. Yes, I'm talking about the love of my life.

Obviously, this story is tender to me because it involves my wife. It is tender to me as well because I am invested with her in this noble cause. Yet what also stirs me and the reason I've placed this tale as the final one in this book, is that the Uncaged story is very much the fruit of all the stories you've read here.

You see, as you'll discover in these next few pages, Kim has been at my side during much of the Westfall Gold story. She has been an executive in our firm and has had a profound impact on its success. She knows the stories. They've imprinted themselves on her heart as they have mine. It has changed her. Prior to this, she had already led magnificently in a variety of arenas, but now we can see that this was God's preparation for the ultimate investment of her life.

What I am saying, then, is that this story—unfinished as it is—is the fruit of all the stories we have seen and many more. So this powerful, moving, still-to-be-written tale is the perfect capstone to what we've seen.

My beautiful wife, Kim, grew up the daughter of a pastor. Because of his unique work, Kim spent her early years in places like Hong Kong and Canada. As with other heroic souls we've seen, having an early life that merged ministry, travel, and a wide variety of cultures left Kim adventurous, curious, and a bit of a nonconformist. I don't mean this in the sense that she is rebellious or angry but rather that she has had the courage to walk her own gentle path, to follow her sense of God's leading even if it meant stepping off the traditional, well-worn road.

At the age of nineteen, then, rather than go to college, Kim bought a franchise, a little gourmet cookie and coffee shop. This was business school the hard way. She learned every aspect of running her own company, from leading people to mastering the hard sciences of accounting and stock management. She was a success, but it wasn't all she was made to do, and she knew it.

She remembers constantly praying that God would give her something great to do for him. And it came. Through circumstances I don't need to describe in detail here, she came into contact with a mission among African orphans called Watoto. You'll learn a bit more about this marvelous organization in the next chapter. Suffice it to say that Kim lost her heart to the beautiful African children and to the exceptional work Watoto does.

The Watoto model is very community oriented and "on the ground." Children aren't warehoused in facilities by Westerners who come from a distance. Instead, the staff live among the children and enter their lives at a deep and transforming level. Kim threw herself into this work and it changed her. I still see the wonderful results of those years in her character and grace all these decades later.

Kim's gifts caused her to rise, as they always do. She became Watoto's executive director for the United States. She coordinated fund-raising, managed programs, and spent years taking groups from the United States to Uganda to help build homes and develop facilities. In one of the most memorable seasons of her life, she coordinated a tour for a Ugandan children's choir that traveled all over the United States to share the good work Watoto was doing and to help Americans gain a vision for the needs of children like those in the choir.

If you ever meet my wife, you will find her to be one of the sweetest and gentlest of creatures. Her laugh is infectious, as is her gift for encouragement. What is not obvious when you meet her is her experience with some of the most ghastly, grisly scenes imaginable. If you work with orphans in Africa, you are going to work with children who have been trafficked for sex from the earliest years of their lives. You're going to confront what can only be described as a modern, underground slave market. And you are going to help children who were left on garbage dumps with their hands tied behind their backs. Yes, I mean literally dumped like garbage. You can't turn away. You can't let your revulsion show. You have to be tough in your compassion, fierce in your love.

This is my wife, Kim.

Her Watoto years rocked on successfully, and then she married me. It is a testimony to her breadth of gifts that when she stepped into our firm, she quickly saw what others of us hadn't seen. We had a smart model that was working for us, particularly when it came to our trademark Donor Weekends, but we didn't see something that Kim realized almost immediately.

We were an organization devoted to excellence, and we set high standards for every part of the services we provided. Yet when we worked with clients, we left nearly all the administration of our events in their hands. It was overwhelming. In a sense, we set the vision and established the benchmarks, but we left the administrative execution to the firms we worked with. It was too much.

Kim saw this, explained it to us, and helped us adjust the model. Rather than leave the execution with our clients, we brought the administrative responsibilities in-house. Kim guided us in this and helped rework our systems. The results were thrilling. The quality of the administration rose, our clients were freed to focus on what they did best, and we immediately saw increased success. Again, this was all due to Kim and her gifts—gifts that had been honed through years of leadership and management.

Now, I've given you all this background on Kim because I want you to see how God works. He often prepares us for what we are made to do by having us do completely different things. You remember the famous scene from *The Karate*

Kid? Mr. Miyagi is training the young Daniel for a karate tournament. But he has the boy waxing and dewaxing old cars first. It doesn't seem to make any sense until we learn that the hand movements for "wax on, wax off" are the same hand movements Daniel will need (Spoiler alert!) to win his tournament.

It's the same with us. God is preparing us through all our experiences, though it rarely ever looks like it.

In Kim's case, the years of preparation came to a culmination at an unexpected time. Kim had "retired"—she's far too young to have retired, so I put this in quotes!—from Westfall Gold and should have been looking forward to some glorious years. She could do whatever she wanted, from traveling to playing with grandchildren to picking up a sport. In other words, she was freer than she had ever been in her life.

This is when it all began. While enjoying her rest from her years of work, Kim kept hearing these words: "children in cages." No, an angel didn't appear, and no audible voice sounded from heaven as in a 1950s Hollywood Bible movie. It was simply the way words form in our hearts when God is speaking, the still, small voice within. Kim couldn't avoid the words. They kept sounding in her soul: "children in cages."

Typical of my wife, she started digging up information. Are there really children in cages in our world? The answer, she discovered to her horror, was yes! There are over forty million men, women, and children being trafficked for sex or labor today, and only about 1 percent of them ever have a chance of being rescued.

The details get so vile that I can't go too far with them on this page. Here is a broad statistic for you, though. The U.S. Justice Department tells us that the average age a girl gets involved in the sex trade through pornography, stripping, or prostitution is thirteen years old. Think of it. Thirteen. Some girls are sold by their families. Some are kidnapped. Yes, some are even taken from shopping malls in the United States, and these are no less or more tragic situations than those that are occurring in millions of episodes elsewhere in the world.

The more Kim learned, the more she was incensed and the stronger the inner voice sounded within. She knew she wanted to make a difference, but the question was how. Human trafficking is a global network of evil that reaches into nearly every part of nearly every nation on earth. How do you make a difference? Where do you begin? You can battle it in court. You can do the dangerous work of rescuing the girls from the traffickers. You can consult with governments in antitrafficking measures. You can incite corporations to work against trafficking and challenge airlines and hotel chains to teach their employees what to watch for. There are a thousand ways to battle against this hydra-headed monster. But which one was Kim's?

Through a series of events, which I'll let Kim tell you

about herself when you attend one of her events, she came to two conclusions. First, it was working with the survivors where she could lead a meaningful effort. She learned that when women are rescued from trafficking, they often have nowhere to go. They need help. They need restoration. They are wounded and deformed of soul. They need time and love and care. Where does it happen? Usually nowhere, and that is why the vast majority of these women end up right back in trafficking.

Kim quickly realized that she wanted to build facilities around the world where the survivors of trafficking could be loved, healed, restored, trained, and set free to live the lives they were made for. The cages needed to be unlocked. These survivors needed to be set free. Kim had to rally people to be the key that unlocks the cage. She decided to call the new organization built for this purpose by an appropriate name: Uncaged! Together, they would develop a global network of high-quality trafficking restoration facilities and see thousands and eventually millions of people truly set free.

Here is where Kim's amazing skills kicked in. She formed a board of leading writers, thinkers, producers, and activists. She also started working with an architectural firm on just the right model for the facilities she hoped to build around the world. They would be called Sanctuaries. She consulted leading experts in the therapies for sexual abuse, and she got them in the same room with the architects to make sure all was done wisely. Then she used her well-honed ability to team people of diverse gifts, and she held summits so that law enforcement could talk to therapists, architects could talk to special forces rescuers, and artists could talk to survivors.

So the work is unfolding. The funds are being raised. The teaming continues.

I can tell you frankly as Kim's husband that it is sobering to watch your wife invade a stronghold of darkness. Keep in mind that while I'm celebrating Kim's gifts with joy in these pages, everything I'm describing is done in the face of a murderous network of criminals. There is a fear factor. There is a constant need to summon the courage. Listen to what Kim herself told our team not long ago:

> I remember that I was sitting in the back seat of a car in Eastern Europe, and I was suddenly faced with the realization I was confronting organized crime head on. I was struck with incredible fear in that moment. I realized that I was about to go to sleep in a hotel room by myself that night and that there were people in the world involved in trafficking who could easily find me and slit my throat. Still, I thought about Queen Esther and how she didn't give in to her fear. I thought about the many signs of confirmation we had been given as we started on this journey. That night, I don't even remember laying my head on my pillow. I woke up at 7:30 a.m. having had one of the best nights of sleep ever. This is what the

battle looks like. This is also what God's breakthroughs look like.

As you can imagine, I'm so very proud of Kim. I'm also being forced to a whole new level of care and prayer for her. But let me tell you why it is all worth it.

There is a young lady somewhere in Eastern Europe. We're going to call her Anna. That's not her name. She was sold into trafficking when she was two years old and by her own family if you can believe it. She then was "used" in a Western European country for years. Finally, through means I shouldn't disclose, Kim and the people she works with got Anna out. Now this precocious little girl has been adopted by a fine family. There is love. There is belonging. And her personality is flowering. After she was rescued, she was so traumatized that she wouldn't talk. Now she giggles and jokes and plays. She's doing well in school and has every promise of a happy, fulfilling life.

Anna's story is possible only because someone unlocked the cage. Someone was the key. I've heard Kim say that she wishes she could say to the millions of Annas still captive in trafficking networks, "We are coming! We have a place for you. We will help set you truly free."

This story is unfinished, although Uncaged recently reached its first mountaintop by establishing a 224-acre sanctuary in Romania. Other older organizations I work with, such as Mercy Ships and Convoy of Hope, are on their tenth mountaintop. But their stories aren't finished either. They all have so much more they want to do.

In every case, I will tell you that because I have seen so much in my years of doing this work, I trust in God. I trust in the power of the Parable of the Talents. I trust in what good people can do. And of course, I trust in my magnificent wife. I believe one day we will see Uncaged establish Sanctuaries all over the world. I believe we will see vast numbers of people delivered from one of the great evils of our age.

Now, I'm always happy to celebrate Kim, but that is not the main reason I have told her story and the story of Uncaged here. I have told it so it can impact you. I want you to see how God prepares people. I want you to see the struggles. I want you to see a God-given vision that is being hammered out but is yet incomplete. I want you to be encouraged that all you might confront as you invest your gifts is being confronted by other people just like you.

Stand strong. Be courageous. Defy the fear. Invest your gifts. Heed the call. A day of victory is coming. And joy awaits you.

Chapter 9

Five Truths for Your Journey

When I stand before God at the end of my life, I would hope that I would not have a single bit of talent left, and could say, "I used everything you gave me."

—Erma Bombeck

I want you to know, now that we've reached the final chapter in this book, that I've been where you are. I've heard the truths you've read in these pages. I've had the spotlight of God focused on my soul. I've had to make the decisions that you now face. In other words, I understand.

So I have some final thoughts for you, some wisdom that I trust will serve you well. I trust this will meet you where you are, show you that you are not alone, and help you take the next steps God has called you to take.

First, I want you to know that there is always an element

of fear in such things. There is always a need to more tightly grasp our faith in God.

I remember hearing Larry Page, founder of Google, say something about his team being so afraid that Google might fail that they thought about not even starting the company.

Notice the words: "so afraid." I've felt this way. I imagine you have too. Yet the fact is that when we are *led* to do something—when we feel God *urging us on* to do that one thing only we have the creativity, compassion, desire, or talent to do—all our fears of failure must be thrown aside. All the naysayers must be ignored. All the impossible odds must not dishearten us. And all the dependence upon ourselves must be relinquished.

Let me ask you a question. Do you believe—really believe—the statement from the Bible that says, "Unless the Lord builds the house, they labor in vain who build it; unless the Lord guards the city, the watchman keeps awake in vain" (Ps. 127:1)? Do you believe that he is the mighty one who trains your hands for battle so that your arms can bend a bow of bronze (2 Sam. 22:35)?

It is not up to you and me to worry about results. It is up to you and me to figure out what God wants us to do— and to do it. If he is with you in the dream he has placed in your heart, nothing can stop it from unfolding the way he wants it to, no matter how impossible it may seem.

Second, take this truth and make it your own: God has already given you what you need. He has *already given you* the talent, ability, skill, money, or passion you need to fulfill his plan, to be entrusted with more, and to walk in pure joy. That's one of the key truths of the Parable of the Talents that many people miss.

Remember?

The master went on a journey. But before he left, he called his servants in and "entrusted his possessions to them" (Matt. 25:14b). He passed out five talents to one, two to another, and one to a third, "each according to his own ability," and then he went on his way.

What I'm trying to show is that you *already have* everything you need! The skill is within you. The dream is inside you. The plan is in place. The passion is there. The ability is woven into your DNA by the Creator himself.

Have you examined your life? The people within your circles? The possibilities within your realm?

That young man I visited in Texas had overlooked his two coworkers and the two couples in his Sunday school class. They were right under his nose!

Will you be faithful in the little things? Examine your life today.

Don't make the mistake of saying, "When I have more time, I'll pursue that dream," or, "When I have more money, I'll give to this or that organization." No. We have to get our eyes focused on the central issues. What are your "talents"? What were you designed to do before the earth started turning?

Something beckons you, calls your name, burns within. It matters not if you're a doctor or teacher, mother or father, executive or electrician, student or senior, pastor or painter, decorator or doorman, spouse or single, entrepreneur or assembly line worker.

We are each "His workmanship, created in Christ Jesus for good works, which God prepared beforehand, that we should walk in them" (Eph. 2:10).

What God values most is the return we bring on the investment he's left with us. If you're a busy individual, like most of us, let me encourage you to take a moment to stop everything else you might be doing right now, get alone, get quiet, and answer a few potentially life-changing questions.

But before you do that, I invite you to ask God for his wisdom and insight as you answer these questions. Ask him what he expects of you. Ask him to help you understand the talents he has invested into your life. And ask him to help you understand how to double those talents and bring him a magnificent return. Perhaps you can form these words into a life-changing prayer:

> For if you cry for discernment, lift your voice for
> understanding;
> If you seek her as silver, and search for her as for
> hidden treasures;
> Then you will discern the fear of the Lord,
> and discover the knowledge of God.

For the Lord gives wisdom;
from his mouth come knowledge and understanding.
  (Prov. 2:3–6)

Third, I have to bring you back to the joy factor. It is one of the most transforming truths I know.

Whether you're a parent or not, you can imagine how it feels to invest endless hours, resources, and physical and mental energy into your children, trying to instill godly morals and values into their lives. Being the father of four, I can tell you, parenting is a tiring and often thankless job. As Dr. James Dobson says, parenting definitely isn't for cowards!

Yet there is an incomparable, almost indescribable feeling that can result in the process of parenting. And that happens when your children are obedient, when, with the unquestioning faith only a child possesses, they remember what you've taught them and simply put it into practice.

Your little boy halts at the curb to watch for traffic when a ball is kicked into the street.

Your little girl hurries to help her brother when he falls from his bicycle.

Your son tells the truth in a heated situation.

Your teenage daughter says she's not going to that sleepover because many of the girls are gossips.

Your college graduate says he's going to work for a non-profit that helps high-risk, inner-city children.

Imagine the emotions you experience as a parent. Pure joy. Not the joy you experienced when you got your first puppy or that came with your first kiss. Not a roller coaster joy that lasts only a few moments. I'm talking about a joy that is so deep-seated, so beyond mere emotion, that it rises up from the very core of your being and permeates your mind and soul.

It's a joy that no one can steal and nothing can extinguish. It's a joy that embodies you and was created specifically for you by the author and Creator of your life. The joy of which I speak is the very essence of a fulfilled life. Jesus said, "Whoever finds his life will lose it, and whoever loses his life for my sake will find it" (Matt. 10:39).

The Bob Westfall translation of that says that when you live for yourself, you never find the true meaning of life; you never experience pure joy. But when you give yourself up for God's use and invest your talents for his purpose, then you find the true meaning of life—and abundant joy.

It's what you were meant for.

Our Creator experiences that same joy when you and I invest what he has entrusted to us in ways that produce fruit.

"His master said to him, 'Well done, good and faithful servant. You were faithful with a few things, I will put you in charge of many things; *enter into the joy of your master*'" (Matt. 25:23; emphasis mine).

I believe it is what we do with the "talents" God has given us that determines the joy in our lives. Likewise, it is what we *do not* do with those talents that can set our lives on a different course.

Fourth, it just could be that God is going to build on the success you already have. I want to say this clearly to you in case God seems to be leading you this way.

Consider the story of my friends Gary and Marilyn Skinner. They were missionaries in Africa and had founded a church in Kampala, Uganda, called Watoto Church. They labored and the church grew from next to nothing to eighteen thousand members. That's a huge church!

Yet then God prompted Gary to reach out to the scores of widows and orphans in the area. As Gary tells it, "I told God, 'Lord, I came here to run this church.'"

But God told him, "You need to reach out to the widows and orphans."

"No, God," Gary responded. "I'm here to run this big church. You know that."

"No," God said. "You're here to reach out to the widows and orphans of this community."

"But I don't want to deal with snotty-nosed, big-bellied, fly-in-the-eye children!"

"But that's what I've built you to do." And so Watoto Child Care Ministries was born.

Since its inception, the ministry has rescued more than five thousand orphans from lives of despair. They have helped more than four thousand vulnerable women live lives of dignity. They have also sent over one hundred choirs across six continents to declare the love of God and plead the cause of poverty-plagued children.

One of the features of Watoto I love the most is the way they build children's villages that consist of 35 to 150 homes. They place each orphaned child in a home with one housemother—usually a widow—and eight other children. It becomes their "forever family." The belonging and human connections that thrive in these homes change lives and redirect destinies. These children are loved, they are taught, they are mentored, and they are given vision for their futures. I believe that out of those homes will come Africa's future leaders.

In addition to these homes, Watoto also builds schools, medical clinics, and community centers/churches, and they create self-sustainability through farming. For the children, unconditional love and spiritual mentoring abound. The physical needs of the children are met, and they are equipped with moral values and life skills that will enable them to lead lives of significance and become leaders and agents of change. But Gary and Marilyn's ministry doesn't stop in Africa. Amazingly, thirty-seven such villages have been built around the world!

Visiting an orphanage where her mom worked in China, my wife, Kim, was struck by the way the parentless little ones reached out to her for human contact. "It was one of the worst days of my life," Kim recalls. "Seeing those poor kids, my heart was gripped. I was a wreck, in tears. Couldn't stop thinking about their need for the love of a mom and dad and how desperate they were for human affection." That vivid memory never left Kim, and she went on to manage the U.S. office for Watoto Child Care Ministries, as I described in our last chapter.

Do you see how Gary and Marilyn took the talents and abilities God gave them and faithfully invested them in others? The return has been unfathomable—and priceless. Yet notice that the Lord used the foundation of Gary and Marilyn's prior success to build new directions of investment and impact. It may be the same for you.

Finally, as you launch into this journey, remember to build a culture of generosity in all that your life touches. Let me tell you about a family that does this beautifully. We'll call them the Smiths. They are living out a legacy of giving received from generations past and passing a greater one on to generations that will follow, beginning with their four children.

The family operates an electronics firm in the Midwest. They are highly successful. Yet my focus is not so much on what they do professionally or what they have earned. It is what they have done with what they've earned.

Both parents in the Smith family came from modest backgrounds but also from people who were great givers. The dad recalls that his grandfather and grandmother were constantly giving to those in need, to missionaries in particular. In fact, the family often gave up Christmas presents so that they could give to others. The parents would simply explain to the children the biblical truth that the family had been blessed to be a blessing, not for their own sake. And so they gave and gave sacrificially.

They live out this legacy today, and they have fun doing it. One favorite family practice is what they call the "grocery run." They fill bags with food and provisions to take to a needy family. Then they put these bags on the front porch of the folks in need, ring the doorbell, and run away to watch from a hiding place. The joy and tears of gratitude they see are their greatest reward.

Today, the Smiths' companies have thrived, and there is great wealth to pass along. Yet they continue pressing the lessons of generosity into the hearts of their young. Years ago, the family decided that if any of the children had a cause they wanted the family to give to, the family's foundations would give twenty times whatever the child gave if it was approved. First, though, that child had to make a presentation to the whole family to convince them of the worthiness of the cause. So a nine-year-old grandson, for example, would have to study and prepare to make an engaging presentation to convince the rest of the family that they should serve the cause dear to his heart. Imagine what this is building in the lives of the family's young children.

Of course, given how God works, this culture of generosity brings its own pressures for growth. When the children in the family were young, they were only able to give ten or twenty dollars to a cause. The foundation would then give twenty times that amount. When the children got older and could give hundreds of dollars at a time, the gifts got larger and larger. This has continued through the years since. Now the Smith family is committed to giving more than $100 million through their foundation in the years to come.

How is it they can give so much? Because as the Bible tells us, "The generous man prospers." This family has lived out the Parable of the Talents over and over again. They have prospered, and they fully understand that they have prospered not just for themselves but to bless others throughout the world.

And here is what excites me. The Smiths have built such a culture of generosity in their family that their children, their grandchildren, and even Smith generations yet unborn will grow up in this culture of generosity and live it out in their time.

This, my friends, is how we change the world. We build a culture of generosity in our lives and spread its reach as far as we can.

Epilogue

As we finish out our time together in these pages, I can't help but hold up everything we've seen together against the truth of Christ's return. In fact, I think this is one of the most powerful truths contained in the Parable of the Talents.

It is pretty obvious that Jesus was speaking symbolically about himself when he said that a man was about to go on a long journey. It's a journey that culminates with him seated on his throne. One day, he will return just as he describes in the Parable of the Talents, and today he says to each of us, "When I return, I want to know how you spent your time, what you did with your talents, and what you did with my possessions that I entrusted into your hands."

This excites me. At the same time, it sobers me.

We don't see God with our natural eyes now, but we do have his Word, the Bible. Do we believe it? Does he tell us he's coming back? Is he serious about what he expects us to be doing while he is away? Is he going to reward us when he gets here, or possibly punish us?

The answer is yes! The Lord of judgment is coming back. And when Christ returns, he will settle accounts:

"Look, I am coming soon! My reward is with me, and I will give to each person according to what they have done" (Rev. 22:12 NIV).

Notice that the first thing on Christ's mind when he speaks of his return is rewarding those who have done well, used their time wisely, and invested the talents he's given. The Scriptures indicate that he can't wait to get here to pay us back for our diligent work on his behalf.

I want you to deeply feel this truth in the parable. So imagine with me for a moment. Picture yourself about to go on a long journey. You are going to be gone so long it simply doesn't make sense to keep your most prized possessions stored up in a rental facility. So you go to three investors and make them a proposal: "Will you manage these possessions for me while I am away?" You give one person $50,000, another $20,000, and another $10,000.

You are gone for many years. Then you come home, and you meet with your investors to find out what kind of returns they've made on your money. The first one hands you $100,000! "What?" you say. "Are you serious? Thank you so much! That is incredible. Wow! The next time I leave, I will give you more to manage. I am so happy with you. This fills me with joy. And you should be happy, too, because you have exceeded my expectations."

After similar positive results with the second investor, we skip to the third man, who simply says, "Here is the $10,000 you asked me to take care of for you."

"What?" you say, flabbergasted. "Are you kidding me? You didn't buy stocks or bonds or mutual funds or even put the money in a CD so I could have gained a little interest? Give me that $10,000! I'm giving it to the one who earned me $50,000; I know he will do something of value with it."

There is a profound principle here, my friend. When we invest wisely and devoutly in the talents God has given us, he gives us more. When the servant who buried his money returned the talent he was given, that talent was immediately given to the one who had doubled the master's five talents:

> Therefore take away the talent from him, and give it to the one who has the ten talents. For to everyone who has shall more be given, and he will have an abundance; but from the one who does not have, even what he does have shall be taken away. (Matt. 25:28, 29)

When do we receive our rewards for investing well? Not until heaven? Could it be that we experience rewards from heaven here on earth for our good stewardship of God's resources? Just ask some of the people featured in this book.

How does Sean Lambert feel each time he gives a poor family the key to a new home? Or Don Schoendorfer when a disabled elderly woman sits in one of his wheelchairs for the first time? What do you suppose Hal Donaldson feels as the cause he built feeds thousands of children every day? Or Burt Rosen, welcoming four hundred people every night?

I know because they've told me. It is joy. It is reward. It is complete fulfillment. I want you to have this reward too.

A final thought for you. In the Parable of the Talents, we are told that the two men who made sure their talents increased did something very specific. Here are the first two sentences of that parable to help you see it:

> He who had received the five talents went at once and traded with them, and he made five talents more. So also he who had the two talents made two talents more.

It says very clearly that both men "went at once." They didn't delay. They didn't say, "I'll wait a few years to see what happens." No, they got on it. They got busy. They "went at once."

If you've been with me through the journey of this book, then you've been considering what your gifts and talents are. You've been pondering what you've been entrusted with that is meant to be used for good in the world, which is meant to be maximized. Take the time you need to think and pray and consult with those who should be part of such decisions in your life. Then act! Don't wait. Once you are sure, nothing good comes of delay. Take the step of courage and make the investment. People are waiting. Needs are waiting.

And a greater joy than you've ever known is waiting to flood into your life.

Victories Yet to Come

In our time together in these pages, we've learned the founding stories of some amazing organizations. We've tracked the personal journeys of those called to change the lives of millions of people, and we've learned a bit about their struggles and victories. Yet there are more victories to come. More of the story to be written. More lives to be transformed. And perhaps you play a role!

I want to urge you to keep following the impact of the heroic organizations we've explored together. You'll be moved by what God is doing and inspired to invest your talents just as boldly. You simply won't be the same.

WestfallGold.com   KARM.org

MercyShips.org   OneCollective.org

YWAMHomesofHope.org   Amazima.org

FreeWheelchairMission.org   Uncaged.org

Cure.org   Watoto.com

ConvoyofHope.org

Acknowledgments

Kim, you stood with me in battles. Some people might have given up, but you stayed the course. You have loved through unloving conditions, and you have done so with grace, patience, and kindness. You were the inspiration for my journey as an author. On top of that, you are the world's best bonus mom and grandmother. Thank you.

To Alan Gold, thank you for throwing your life and skills into the vision of Westfall Gold. I appreciate your creative genius, your remarkable sense of humor, and your straight-shooting wisdom. You are a friend indeed.

To our dear friends Stephen and Beverly Mansfield, thank you for forcing me to pursue the vision of *The Courage Factor*. For your publishing wisdom, tireless encouragement, and deep commitment to the fulfillment of this dream, I thank you.

To Henry and Tori Cloud, you have believed in us from the very beginning. You have stood with us, laughed with us, and consumed mounds of jalapeño potato chips with us. And of course, on the more serious side, you have been incredibly loving friends.

To Melissa Butler, you amaze me so much! You managed

this project with grace, passion, conviction, and excellence. Thank you.

To Lauren Gaither, Glen Slattery, and Steffen Smith, our Westfall Gold senior writers, thank you for your thorough assistance in research and information gathering while smack in the middle of the busiest season. Your encouragement, professionalism, and care shine throughout this book.

Brittni, Jessica, Austin, and Alyssa, you are incredible, beautiful, kind, and smart. I see the principles in this book beginning to blossom in your lives. I'm honored to be your dad.

Study Guide

The best way to read this book is to read it with others, whether on your team, with a group of friends, or in your church or small group. My recommendation is that each participant read through the whole book and then plan to meet for five weeks to reflect on it all together. Plan to use the note pages for your thoughts or to jot down what others share. I think you will see huge breakthroughs if you'll follow this simple study outline.

—Bob Westfall

Week One: What the Parable of the Talents Means to Me

Read the Parable of the Talents in Matthew 25:14–30. What, in your opinion, is the main overall message in this passage?

Do you believe God has given you some truly unique talents and abilities? According to the Parable of the Talents, what are you supposed to do with those talents and abilities?

In the Parable of the Talents, what do you think the master means when he says, "Enter into the joy of your master"? Is it meant for you, today? How do you attain that?

Are you fulfilled in your current work or occupation? Have you been faithful "in the little things"? Be honest and discuss.

Do you believe God wants you to have joy here on earth?

Notes

Week Two: God's Calling on My Life

We often think about ministers and evangelists as receiving a call to ministry. Does God give "regular people" a calling as well? Why or why not?

Discuss a time in your life when you felt that God was leading you to pursue a calling. What was he asking of you? If you are not pursuing that "calling" or have not received one, what are you doing today that is significant to God?

Do you think that God has you right where he wants you? When is it easy to think this? What makes it challenging?

Pride can sometimes get in the way of accomplishing the things God wants us to accomplish. Has this been true for you? Discuss how pride can be a barrier to flourishing as God would have us.

Notes

Week Three: What Is My Story?

Think about Sean Lambert's trip and Don Schoendorfer's story (both in Chapter Four). Has God ever hit you with a similar, almost overwhelming challenge? Explain and discuss.

What really grips your heart and pulls at your emotions? For my wife, it was seeing an orphanage full of desperate children in China (see Chapter Nine). Could what grips your heart be your calling? What talent—be it treasure or ability or passion or skill—has God entrusted to you today? What passion has he woven into your heart, and only your heart?

Think about the relationships in your life that require you to care for others. How can you give these relationships the energy and attention that they require and deserve?

How are you treating the "ministry" or talent that is yours today—even if it isn't glamorous? How can you better cultivate it?

Notes

Week Four: What Does It Cost?

If the Lord returned today and asked for an account of the "talents" he had entrusted into your life, what could you tell him? What is your "return on investment" or, in this case, "return on talent"? How can our fears cripple God's ability to work in our lives?

The Bible says, "For where your treasure is, there your heart will be also" (Matt. 6:21). Be honest—where is your treasure today? How can you identify what you actually treasure?

Sometimes, in order to invest all the talents God has given you, it requires blind faith. Can you recall examples from the book in which people had to take uncertain risks? Is that true in your case? Discuss.

Discuss this statement: "It is not up to you and me to worry about the results. It is up to you and me to figure out what God wants us to do—and do it."

Notes

Week Five: Is There Anything More?

Have you ever imagined meeting God at the finish line and having to confess, "Master, I was afraid to take the risk and leverage the talents you gave me. I played it safe and stayed within my comfort zone. I kept my status-quo job—the benefits were too good to pass up"? Discuss.

Often, in doing what God wants us to do, there is grunt work involved. It isn't easy, and there are no promises that it will succeed. If this is true of your circumstances, how does that make you feel? How can you overcome that feeling of the tasks or work you are doing being insignificant?

Think about a time in your life when God opened doors of opportunity. What was that like? Whom did he allow you to meet and what did you experience?

Have you ever fallen into the trap of saying, "Someday when I have more money or time, I'll do that"?

Do you believe this statement: God has already given you the talent, ability, skill, or passion you need to fulfill his plan, to be entrusted with more, and to walk in pure joy?

God can create an opportunity in your life that is surprising and even different than the one that you have in mind. That is what happened to Gary Skinner (see Chapter Nine). Has God ever revealed a plan involving you that you simply did not like and that was not part of your plan?

Jesus said, "Whoever finds his life will lose it, and whoever loses his life for my sake will find it" (Matt. 10:39). Discuss this verse and what it means to you as it relates to giving yourself up for God's use.

Notes

About Bob Westfall

Bob launched Westfall Gold in 2002 with a singular mission: to help clients fund transformational impacts around the world. Inspired by the Parable of the Talents, he has drawn on his experience in major donor development to build one of the country's preeminent fund-raising consultancies.

To date, the Westfall Gold team has guided leading universities, nonprofits, and faith-based organizations in raising more than $1 billion—with billions more in their sights!

Bob is a recognized expert in the field of major donor fund-raising and is accredited as a master trainer by the Association of Fundraising Professionals. He also serves as a director of the Giving Institute and is a highly sought-after speaker at leadership and development conferences around the world. Bob admits that his greatest achievement is his family.

His wife, Kim, keeps him anchored and on track. And with four grown children and four grandchildren, they both have their hands full. In his spare time, Bob is divided between the tennis courts and the golf course. For more information about Bob's amazing firm, visit WestfallGold.com.

ABOUT
WESTFALL GOLD

Bob Westfall is the Founder and CEO of Westfall Gold, one of the nation's leading fundraising consultancies. His company has inspired more than a billion dollars in transformational giving to the nation's leading nonprofits. Their innovative "Major Donor Experience" bonds donors to the organization's vision by creating the case, inspiring trust, and building community—forging strategic partnerships that last a lifetime.

WESTFALL GOLD

For more, visit www.westfallgold.com, email info@westfallgold.com, or call 678-730-0844.